T0328703

Cambridge Elements ☰

Elements in Business Strategy
edited by
J.-C. Spender
Kozminski University

STRATEGIZING WITH INSTITUTIONAL THEORY

Harry Sminia
Strathclyde Business School

CAMBRIDGE
UNIVERSITY PRESS

CAMBRIDGE
UNIVERSITY PRESS

Shaftesbury Road, Cambridge CB2 8EA, United Kingdom

One Liberty Plaza, 20th Floor, New York, NY 10006, USA

477 Williamstown Road, Port Melbourne, VIC 3207, Australia

314–321, 3rd Floor, Plot 3, Splendor Forum, Jasola District Centre, New Delhi – 110025, India

103 Penang Road, #05–06/07, Visioncrest Commercial, Singapore 238467

Cambridge University Press is part of Cambridge University Press & Assessment, a department of the University of Cambridge.

We share the University's mission to contribute to society through the pursuit of education, learning and research at the highest international levels of excellence.

www.cambridge.org
Information on this title: www.cambridge.org/9781009507660

DOI: 10.1017/9781009357654

First published 2024

A catalogue record for this publication is available from the British Library.

ISBN 978-1-009-50766-0 Hardback
ISBN 978-1-009-35766-1 Paperback
ISSN 2515-0693 (online)
ISSN 2515-0685 (print)

Strategizing with Institutional Theory

Elements in Business Strategy

DOI: 10.1017/9781009357654
First published online: May 2024

Harry Sminia
Strathclyde Business School
Author for correspondence: Harry Sminia, harry.sminia@strath.ac.uk

Abstract: This Element consults seven variants of institutional theory to explore how these can be applied to strategic management. These variants are New Institutional Economics, Old Institutionalism, New Institutionalism, institutional entrepreneurship and change, intra-organizational institutionalization, institutional logics, and institutional work. In doing so, three strategic management styles are distinguished: competitiveness-based strategic management, legitimacy-based strategic management, and performativity-based strategic management. While the competitive-based style sees institutional theory submitting to mainstream strategy research, offering additional variables and considerations to explain competitive advantage, the legitimacy-based style makes institutional theory a strategy theory in its own right by providing an explanation for an organization's viability that emphasizes legitimacy over competitive advantage. The performativity-based style is an even more radical departure from mainstream strategizing by purporting that a future is actively created with organizations making contributions as emerging issues are being dealt with.

Keywords: strategic management, institutional theory, competitiveness, legitimacy, performativity

ISBNs: 9781009507660 (HB), 9781009357661 (PB), 9781009357654 (OC)
ISSNs: 2515-0693 (online), 2515-0685 (print)

Contents

1 Introduction: Applying Institutional Theory to Strategy

For many reasons it is difficult to write about how institutional theory is relevant for strategic management. These include it not being clear what exactly an institution is, what it explains, and how it is to be explained. Some argue that institutional theory is not a theory at all and more a brand with which researchers identify (Alvesson et al., 2019). Rather than taking these reasons as an excuse to declare institutional theory as useless and as having to get its act together, we can take this criticism as indicative of the complex world that organizations must deal with. When we do that, we open up a rich and nuanced understanding of what can be deemed as of 'strategic' importance, or indeed to understand what strategic management is about. Institutional theory not only adds to what we must consider when thinking about the content of our strategies. It also has things to say about the process or management part; about how strategy might be realized or implemented.

Despite the proliferation of definitions of 'institution', there are some common threads. Firstly, institution is an expression of social order; of a regularity in human activity, which tends to occur time and time again. Social order is the bedrock of society. Without social order, society would not exist. Moreover, institution refers to something that is experienced as real yet is largely virtual and intangible; associated with norms, values, understandings, meanings, ideas, and cognitions. For strategic management, institutional theory potentially provides a range of different understandings of how firms and any other types of organization can and must function in society at large. Maurice (1979) described institutions as 'the societal effect'. Moreover, by recognizing that organizations are little societies by themselves, institutional theory has something to say about how these can and must be managed as well.

The proliferation of the many variants of institutional theory that we have is a consequence of the many ways in which ideas have been developed about how to understand society and about how it could and should be governed. The concept of institution is a prominent feature in sociology, economics, and political science. Increasingly, the words 'institution', 'institutional', and 'institutionalization' appear in management and organization theory (Greenwood et al., 2008), often as derivatives or 'borrowings' of theorizing in sociology, economics, and, to a lesser extent, political science.

Secondly, legitimacy is a key term in theorizing about institutions. Again, there are many definitions in existence (Suchman, 1995; Suddaby et al., 2017). As a common thread, legitimacy tries to capture that for an organization to be able to exist and function in society, its activities in some way must be acceptable, suitable, tolerable, effectual, or something of that nature. For business firms, legitimacy compares with the requirement of being competitive or having competitive advantage. Some institutional theorists in management and organ-ization see legitimacy as a contributor to competitive advantage – legitimacy helps a firm to be more competitive. Others see it as an additional requirement – firms must be both competitive and legitimate. And there are those who see competitive advantage as being defined by legitimacy – legitimacy tells what the competition is supposed to be about.

There is also a resemblance with the concept of value in that there are many declarations that organizations must produce value to be economically viable or justified. Value tends to be closely associated with money. What an organization delivers is compared with the costs or the price that has to be paid. Legitimacy tends to rely on a broader justification, albeit money con-siderations often are part of it. The difference is reminiscent of the Oscar Wilde quote about knowing the costs (money) of everything but the value (understood as legitimacy) of nothing, although this comparison might do an injustice to the multi-facedness of the notion of value (cf. Lepak et al., 2007). Nevertheless, organizations – and even business firms – can be considered legitimate without ever making a profit or despite forever exceeding their allocated budgets (Meyer & Zucker, 1989).

There are branches of institutional theory that concentrate more on institu-tionalization than on institutions. Their concern is about how legitimacy is gained and lost, or more fundamentally about how what is legitimate changes, rather than about how to fulfil the requirements of legitimacy as these might exist. These theories offer explanations about how organizations contribute to maintaining societal demands and expectations, how they help changing these to their advantage, or sometimes more altruistically, how people and organiza-tions can make society a better place to live in.

Organizations and especially business firms being actively involved in chan-ging what is seen as legitimate to their advantage points towards a serious ethical concern. To what extent is it right or legitimate for commercial or other partial interests to tell society what is right and what is wrong? Institutional theorists who see competitive advantage as a requirement separate from legitimacy often argue that legitimacy is the responsibility of government whose task is to set out the playing field so that firms then can compete within this (often with an expectation that this government is democratically elected). Institutional theorists who see legitimacy and competitiveness as intertwined do not have it that easy, ending up with theories that not only explain but also take up moral positions.

Legitimacy considerations can be converted into strategic management appli-cations, and indeed some of them already have. Besides, while discussing strategy, managers can find themselves using argumentations that resemble one of the many variants of institutional theory without them knowing it.

In trying to implement strategy, they might be informed by their own – maybe intuitively derived – 'theory-in-use' (Argyris & Schön, 1978), that is the way they understand how they can be effective as a manager. A strategist's theory-in -use could well be a variant of institutional theory.

What this text has on offer is not the ultimate or best institutional theory for strategic management. Instead, it provides an opportunity for readers who are practicing strategists to compare their understanding of strategic management and how they do it, to the translations into the realm of strategy of several prominent but different variants of institutional theory. For researchers, the text delivers an overview of the state-of-affairs regarding institutional theory and its relevance and maybe irrelevance for the field of strategic management. It will also develop some ideas for further research and what interesting research questions would be, at some point even boldly suggesting to re-direct the strategy field towards becoming more sociologically informed.

To get to grips with institutional theory and its applicability in strategic management it is useful to understand that the theorizing is stratified. There is a foundation of basic theories derived from economics like methodological individualism (Von Mises, 1949), or derived from sociology like social construction (Berger & Luckmann, 1966), structuration theory (Giddens, 1984), or actor-network theory (Latour, 2005), which have worked their way into variants of institutional theory like Old Institutionalism (Selznick, 1957), New Institutionalism (DiMaggio & Powell, 1991), institutional logics (Thornton & Ocasio, 2008), or institutional work (Lawrence & Suddaby, 2006), and into more specific institutional theory applications like Non-Market Strategy (Mellahi et al., 2016), or into International Business/Strategy (Hotho & Pedersen, 2012) and strategic change (Hinings & Greenwood, 1988a).

The text will trace these lineages, starting with economics-derived New Institutional Economics and its applications in strategy. This will be followed by exploring the more sociological variants and their basic theoretical roots as well as their (potential) application into strategy. Often enough, there is a clearly recognizable ancestry from basic theory to strategy application, aided by academic texts referencing the associated literature. Nevertheless, in many cases, there is more reading between the lines required to make the connections, having to rely on recognizing similar argumentation that appears in basic theory, in management and organization theory and research, and in strategy applications. Referencing and mutual criticizing does provide many clues about where authors get their ideas from. Albeit some contributions are a bit promiscuous, combining ideas with different parentage.

A complication in making all these variants of institutional theory relevant for strategic management is the presumption of agency that is built into the notion of strategy. Strategic management assumes a strategist to have 'strategic choice' (Child, 1972); to have sufficient command over the process by which an organization performs to be able to direct this process towards a desired outcome. From an institutional theory point of view, this presumption of agency is problematic because the very notion of institution proclaims that something extra-individual imposes social order on to this process, determining how this process proceeds towards maybe different outcomes than the strategist had intended. Within institutional theory, this complication started being referred to as the 'paradox of embedded agency' (Holm, 1995; Seo & Creed, 2002). Alternative variants of institutional theory differ from each other regarding what is proposed as a solution to this paradox, or whether this is made a point of at all.

Each variant of institutional theory has different presumptions of how process proceeds, or as it will be referred to in this text: process principles. That is, among the many layers in every alternative version of institutional theory there is a specific presumed process philosophy of how process progresses, from which the extent of presumed agency or strategic choice can be derived. These process principles can be traced back to basic theories like methodological individualism, social construction, structuration theory, or actor-network theory, which underpin the many variants of institutional theory. Moreover, different process principles have different ideas about what animates the process, or what is the *deus ex machina* that make it 'go'. The main objective of specifying the process principles is to recognize the distinctions and what each variant has to say about strategic management.

This is expected to help not only in understanding how and why different institutional theories are different, but also to recognize how a strategist's theory-in-use compares and to add to a strategist's repertoire of different ways by which strategic problems can be appreciated and dealt with. A similar usefulness is envisioned for the researcher in that demarcating the differences between as well as the lineages of the many conversations in the field can point the way forward towards interesting future research questions in relation to strategic management. What is deemed impossible is to synthesize everything into one 'grand' institutional theory. The fundamental differences are just too large.

The relevance of institutional theory will be assessed on the basis of a depiction of the strategy process that distinguishes between three different spheres (Sminia, 2022) (see Figure 1). In its broadest sense, there is a process of firms and organizations surviving and being successful in a larger environment. The textbook understanding in the strategy field is that this sphere is characterized by competition and that survival and success depends on having competitive advantage (cf. Barney, 1986; Porter, 1980).

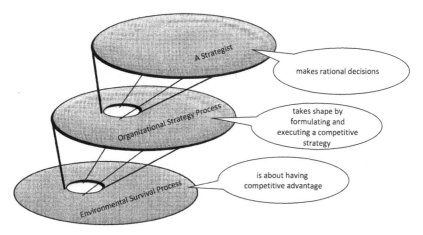

Figure 1 Textbook strategizing.

Zooming into the detail of this environmental survival process there are all these firms and organizations each engaging in their own organizational strategy process, expecting that this somehow will aid the organization's success and survival. The textbook recommendation for this sphere is that there should be a form of explicit strategic planning in place by which a strategy is formulated (cf. Ansoff, 1965). Ideally, such a plan should describe how the organization should position itself in the competitive environment, how the organization's unique capabilities pose a competitive advantage that allows for this positioning, and how this positioning should be executed.

Zooming in even more, there are people – individual strategists – who contribute their thinking and acting to the organizational strategy process. In this third sphere, the textbook strategist is depicted as a rational decision-maker who processes all the relevant information to make the right choices. Realizing a strategy then is a matter of executing a plan (cf. Hrebiniak & Joyce, 1984), of designing and structuring an organization, of putting the right culture and people in place, of acquiring the finance and investments needed, and of monitoring key performance indicators (cf. Kaplan & Norton, 1996) to check whether the implementation is on track.

In a way, sketching out strategic management as a planning process that deals with competition is a bit of a caricature, yet is still the dominant theory-in-use with strategy practitioners as well as with many strategy scholars. Most of the strategy textbooks are written around and endorse this model. It is the distinction between the three spheres of the environmental survival process, the organizational strategy process, and the activities of the individual strategist which will help with pinpointing how various variants of institutional theory have questioned and changed how each sphere can be understood. In doing so, the traditional planning model and the problematization of strategy as being about competitive advantage has been amended or on occasion completely dismissed, although there are instances where the planning model has been maintained with contributions being offered accordingly. What we will end up with is not only an appreciation that there is much more to strategic management than what the basic textbook model tells us. Applying institutional theory to strategy also tells us how basic the textbook model is.

There already are various overviews of institutional theory. These either describe the intellectual development over time (Glynn & D'Aunno, 2023; Scott, 1987) or attempt to provide a synthesis (Micelotta et al., 2017; Scott, 2014).[1] There also are earlier attempts at describing how institutional theory can be made relevant for strategic management (Ingram & Silverman, 2002; Raynard et al., 2016; Smets et al., 2015a; Suddaby et al., 2013). The attempts to make institutional theory relevant for strategy tend to concentrate on one or just a few variants of institutional theory. The overviews do not relate institutional theory specifically to strategy. This text fills that gap. It works its way through all variants that can be made useful for strategy. These are New Institutional Economics, Old Institutionalism, New Institutionalism, institutional entrepreneurship and change, intra-organizational institutionalism, institutional logics, and institutional work. There is some arbitrariness in how the different variants of institutional theory have been distinguished. It follows the precedents set by previous overviews but also was led by the distinctive contributions to strategy by which different variants can be characterized.

Each of these institutional theory variants will be treated to a concise description of how it came about, what it tries to explain, how this explanation is provided, the underlying process principles, and how it develops the notion of institution. Table 1 provides an initial, yet course, overview. From this, the application of each variant to strategic management is developed by indicating what it has to say about the environmental survival process, the organizational strategy process, and the strategist. With some variants, applications have already been developed or research in the strategy field has referenced them, and this will be made use of. This concerns Non-Market Strategy, some research in international business/strategy, research on strategic change, and some research under the Strategy-as-Practice banner. Particular attention will be given to what each variant does with the notion of 'strategic choice' because this is so pivotal for the whole idea of strategic management.

---

[1] The first version of this book appeared as Scott (1992).

Table 1 Overview of Institutional Theory Variants

	Process Principals	Institution	Agency	Process animated by	Provides explanation of
New Institutional Economics	methodological individualism	rules of the game	individual choice with cognitive limitations	efficiency	economic exchange
Old Institutionalism	methodological individualism	an organization infused with value	leadership within negotiated compromise	meaning	whether an organization is an institution or a bureaucracy
New Institutionalism	social construction	norms and values outside organizations	determined by norms and values	compliance	isomorphism/how an organization behaves
Institutional entrepreneurship	structuration theory	regular and recurrent activity patterns	implied by the duality of structure	reflexivity	episodic institutional change
Intra-organizational institutionalization	structuration theory/ sensemaking	an organization's interpretative scheme	implied by the duality of structure	reflexivity	incremental change alternated with strategic change
Institutional logics	institutional logics perspective	an institutional logic	distributed among many actors	individual reflection	heterogeneity/accommodation of institutional complexity
Institutional work	structuration theory	regular and recurrent activity patterns	implied by the duality of structure	reflexivity	institutional continuity and change
Institutional performative work	actor-network theory/ theory of practice	regular and recurrent activity patterns	agencement	teleoaffectivity	constant institutional becoming

Eventually, some synthesis will be provided by proposing three different strategic management styles as emerging out of the applications of institutional theory to strategy. These are competitiveness-based strategic management, legitimacy-based strategic management, and performativity-based strategic management. Each style provides an outline of how strategy is to be done with which a strategist can compare their own theory-in-use. Each style also is suggestive of further research in the strategy field. More specifically, while the competitive-based style would utilize institutional theory to further develop mainstream strategy research by adding additional variables and considerations for explaining and managing competitiveness, the legitimacy-based style and particularly the performativity-based style have the potential to be developed into much needed alternatives to mainstream strategy research. In this way, institutional theory offers an opportunity for the strategy field to re-think what strategy and strategic management is about.

2 Institutions as Constraints: New Institutional Economics

Economics' dominant neo-classical approach has little room for institutions or arrangements of social order that somehow influence what people do. It assumes a *Homo economicus* or rational actor who is free to make any choice based on information that is equally and universally available for everybody. Thorstein Veblen (1909) was an early dissident voice who argued that people when making economic decisions might not be as rational as assumed. He suggested that economists should develop economic theory assuming that people are creatures of habit. They seldomly make deliberate and rational choices. Instead, they just do what they are used to do, because it is customary or due to tradition. This alternative to neo-classical economics lingered on for quite some time under the label of institutional economics. The basic idea is that habits develop into institutions that tell people what to do and how to do it, rather than them being free to rationally choose what they like.

Douglas North (1986, 1990, 1991) eventually took this on and developed what is now referred to as New Institutional Economics (NIE). He was awarded the Nobel Prize in 1993. His project concentrates on answering the question how economic activity can be explained when we abandon the neo-classical ideal of frictionless exchange. Frictionless exchange is what rational actors do in perfect markets when making buy and sell decisions with all information being available. His basic argument is that economic exchange is far from frictionless, especially because of cognitive limitations in human information processing. Drawing on Herbert Simon (1957), he assumes economic actors are only capable of bounded rationality. To him: 'Individuals make choices based on subjectively derived models that diverge among individuals and the information that actors receive is so incomplete that in most cases these divergent models show no tendency to converge' (17). This lack of convergence is what is responsible for generating uncertainty. People just cannot know how other people will act because everybody thinks differently. In turn, this uncertainty adds transaction costs: the costs of engaging in economic exchange. For economic exchange, some kind of effort is required, which translates into what can be understood as the costs of doing business. To North, economic exchange is far from frictionless.

The reasons why this inherent uncertainty about how other people might think and act adds transaction costs is twofold. One reason is that because of this inherent uncertainty some kind of assessment or measurement is required for both parties in the transaction regarding what is being exchanged. Will the seller deliver value? Will the buyer be able pay up? Before doing the deal, people want to know what they get out of it. They need to put effort, time, money into investigating what they will get. The other reason is the costliness of enforcement. Especially if a deal is not instantaneous but requires a seller to perform for a buyer over an extended period and payment comes in instalments, some form of mutual supervision is required to make sure the seller keeps its promise and the buyer pays up.

The solution to this inherent uncertainty is institutions – which are defined as 'the rules of the game in a society' (North, 1990: 3) – that constrain economic activity. These are rules that prohibit or permit what economic actors can do. This can be a good thing or a bad thing because institutions can be efficient and inefficient. North's (1990) argument is that if there are rules that constrain people's behaviour, uncertainty would diminish. Institutions that accomplish this are considered efficient. Institutions that only manage to complicate economic exchange and add transaction costs are considered inefficient. Moreover, he argues that economic activity cannot exist without institutions.

Institutions as rules of the game and as constraints are either formal or informal. Informal constraints are 'part of the heritage that we call culture' (North, 1990: 37) with culture referred to somewhat simply as 'knowledge, values, and other factors that influence behavior' (citing Boyd & Richardson, 1985: 2). Informal rules are also referred to as being 'embodied in customs, traditions, and codes of conduct' (North, 1990: 6) as well as '(1) extensions, elaboration, and modifications of formal rules, (2) socially sanctioned norms of behavior, and (3) internally enforced standards of conduct' (40). A distinguishing feature that sets them apart from formal rules to North is that informal rules tend to be self-imposed and emerge somewhat spontaneously.

It feels as if North (1990) sees informal rules as all norms and values that have not been formalized, albeit recognizing that formalization is a matter of degree.

Formal rules are explicitly formulated and enforceable, and vary 'from constitu-tions, to statue and common laws, to specific bylaws, and finally to individual contracts' (47). Formal rules exist as and apply to jurisdictions, mostly in the form of a country, with a government and a judiciary ultimately being responsible for formalization and enforcement.

Having proposed why and how institutions as constraints and as rules of the game are essential for economic exchange, North (1990) goes on to explain why some countries are more prosperous than others. This is because institutions in rich countries have developed in a way that makes their institutions efficient and minimize transaction costs. Efficient institutions facilitate economic exchange and therefore economic growth. Poorer countries are hampered by institutions that are inefficient and make economic exchange more difficult, therefore adding transaction costs. In making that argument, the institutions that matter include labour regulation, the justice and judicial system, political rights and civil liber-ties, property rights, taxation policies, the financial system, political stability in general, but also corruption. North (1990) has something to say about firms as well but does not really develop it. He likes to refer to firms as players in a sports game, having to find strategies to win while adhering to the rules of the game.

Oliver Williamson, well-known for developing Transaction Costs Economics (TCE) (Williamson, 1975, 1981), is more specific about how institutions as constraints appear with individual firms. He is also considered a representative of New Institutional Economics. He often refers to John Commons (1934) – another early institutional economist – who proclaimed the transaction as the basic unit of analysis for the economist. Oliver Williamson was awarded the Nobel Prize in 2009. Williamson (2000) proposes to differentiate between four levels of analysis when dealing with institutions to then position firms as playing within the rules of the game at level 3. However, each level from top to bottom constrains the level below while from bottom to top there are presumed feedback effects.

The highest level (1) of analysis is the level of embeddedness (cf. Granovetter, 1985) which Williamson (2000) elaborates by way of referring to North's (1990) informal rules or constraints, also denoted as 'culture'. Williamson (2000) claims that economists have not been able to satisfactorily explain how and why informal institutions appear and take shape.[2] Level 2 is North's (1990) formal rules, with Williamson picking up North's thesis that countries need to get the institutions right, that is, efficient, by having these institutions minimalizing transaction costs. Williamson refers to this as '1st order economizing', and largely the

---

[2] Sociologists might disagree here, albeit admitting that sociology has put forward many different explanations for how culture and institutions appear and change. Moreover, some of the institu-tional theory variants based on sociology presented later explicitly address this question.

responsibility of governments. Level 3 is – in North's (1990) terms – about playing the game within the existing rules. This is for firms to get right to maximize their performance. To Williamson (2000), this is a matter of choosing the appropriate mode of governance in terms of his TCE (Williamson, 1975), which he refers to as 2nd-order economizing. Level 4 then is about resource allocation and employment, and firms organizing themselves according to the appropriate governance mechanism. This is the level of 3rd-order economizing, where Williamson claims that neo-classical economics still applies.

In a way Williamson (2000) positions TCE as a further elaboration of the inherent uncertainty that according to North (1990) frustrates the neo-classical ideal of frictionless economic exchange and which generates transaction costs, and for which efficient institutions as constraints are the solution, although his classic *Markets and Hierarchies* book was published fifteen years earlier. Rather than just bounded rationality, there are several compounded factors that create this inherent uncertainty or, as Williamson (1975) prefers, 'moral hazards'. A moral hazard to him is any reason why an economic exchange might not have been satisfactory for either the seller or the buyer, and therefore will cause market failure.

Moral hazards are present because of the 'human factors' of 'bounded rationality' as with North, but also because of 'opportunism', the 'environmental factors' of 'uncertainty/complexity' and 'small numbers', and because of 'information impactedness', all entrenched within 'atmosphere' (Williamson, 1975). Bounded rationality has already been explained as associated with the cognitive limitations on human information processing. To Williamson, this combines with uncertainty/complexity as the reason why information is always questionable. Opportunism refers to the likelihood that people will cheat if given a chance, which creates uncertainty because you will never know whether they will. The risk is mitigated when you are dealing with many buyers and sellers because the risk of being cheated averages out, but is especially present when there are only small numbers and is particularly pressing in situations of 'asset specificity'. Asset specificity is a situation where that what is exchanged is specific to one buyer and one seller. Information impactedness is about all actors knowing something about the exchange but this not being evenly shared. Consequently, different actors must gather different information to level up, and therefore their transaction costs will be different while they will never know how much information asymmetry is still left. All of this is entrenched in atmosphere. With atmosphere Williamson (1975) appears to express that different actors might appreciate an economic exchange differently, especially with regard to the value of what is being exchanged.

Williamson (1975) goes on to argue that to deal with this uncertainty some form of governance will appear. Governance in a way is an institution of some sort that constraints economic actors and therefore mitigates uncertainty and minimizes transaction costs. For this he assumes there exists a '"natural order" with which governance structures take shape in relation to the attributes of transactions' (Williamson, 1999a: 314). If there are no moral hazards, the neoclassical ideal of frictionless exchange will prevail. Frictionless exchange is the market end of a continuum between markets and hierarchies; with many hybrids appearing in between. What form this hybrid takes or whether we end up at the other end of hierarchy depends on what kind of safeguards to mitigate the moral hazards can be put in place. If no safeguards are possible at all, the hybrid form will be a contract that just incorporates all risk in the price that is agreed. If stipulating safeguards becomes so extensive that you end up with such a detailed specification of what needs to be done and how it must be done, you effectively end up with an organization. If that is the case, you might as well organize yourself into a hierarchy. Hybrids are contracts somewhere between market and hierarchy that specify the exchange in terms of price, risks, and safeguards with the lowest possible transaction costs as the guiding principle. However, Williamson continuously makes the point that contracts are never perfect. His thinking inspired Williamson (1991) initially to claim that rather than competitive advantage, efficiency in terms of minimizing transaction costs should be the main focus of strategy. He later positioned competitive advantage and his efficiency argument as complementary (Williamson, 1999b).

NIE essentially is a variant of institutional theory that explains why economic exchange happens. It is because institutions as constraints alleviate the uncertainty about the outcomes of such economic exchange. NIE also expects that people look for efficiency in terms of minimizing transaction costs. On that basis North (1990, 1991) provides suggestions about how NIE could be relevant for strategic management. In its most general sense, NIE sees the environmental survival process as firms making the most of the 'rules of the game' or the institutions that apply to them, although there are a few hints that firms could also involve themselves with influencing these rules (see Figure 2).

Williamson (1991) initially stipulated that the environmental survival process in strategy should focus on efficiency, but he later relented and declared efficiency and competitive advantage as complementary (Williamson, 1999b). For the efficiency part, strategy should focus on selecting arrangements that minimalize transaction costs with all the economic exchange that an organization is engaged in. This 2nd-order economizing should be followed by 3rd-order economizing of actually putting these governance arrangements in place (Williamson, 2000). This nicely fits with the presumption of the organizational strategy process being a matter of processing information about price, risk, and safeguards, with the strategist seen as a rational decision-maker albeit constrained by limited cognitive

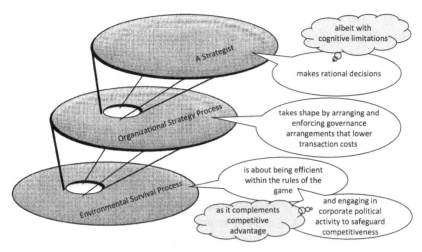

Figure 2 New institutional economics strategizing.

abilities. Strategy realization then happens by drafting and enforcing contracts on the continuum between market and hierarchy.

The underlying process principles of NIE are derived from Methodological Individualism (Von Mises, 1949) – as is the case with much of economics. Methodological Individualism presumes that collective effects like an institution or an organizational outcome ultimately are a consequence of individual choices and motivations. NIE does recognize that individuals when making choices are hampered by their cognitive limitations and other moral hazards, yet still are presumed to make them to the best of their abilities, motivated as they are by utility maximation and transaction costs minimalization. It is efficiency that is taken as ultimately animating the process. Just like gravity always will be moving water downstream despite obstacles getting in the way, efficiency is what drives the process forward in NIE.

Methodological Individualism also informs the conceptualization of the individual strategist as a rational decision-maker. North's and Williamson's theorizing then serves as cognitive aids that help with grasping the complexity of situations to draft and realize strategy. As such, NIE has been picked up by a research stream that has labelled itself as Non-Market Strategy, and by researchers in International Business/Strategy (IB/S).

Non-Market Strategy is establishing itself as a research stream within the strategic management field. It is put forward as something that strategic managers must concern themselves with just as much as with market or competitive strategy. The basic idea is that for a firm the environment is divided into two parts. The competitive environment requires competitive strategy. 'The nonmarket environment includes those interactions that are intermediated by the public, stakeholders, government, the media, and public institutions. These institutions differ from those of the market environment because of characteristics such as majority rule, due process, broad enfranchisement, collective action, and publicness' (Baron, 1995a: 47). The nonmarket environment requires a firm to also have a Non-Market Strategy (Baron, 1995a; Henisz & Zelner, 2003; Mellahi et al., 2016).

Most of the advice that researchers in this realm provide to strategic managers is that firms must engage with government policy to shape the non-market or regulatory environment in a way that their competitive advantage is preserved, if not enhanced. This is what is referred to as 'corporate political activity' (Getz, 1997; Hillman & Hitt, 1999). How exactly strategic managers must do this varies with the country the firm is operating in, but more concrete theorizing and associated advice tend to be somewhat biased towards how it works in the USA (Bonardi et al., 2005; de Figueirdo, 2009; Holburn & Vanden Bergh, 2008; Kingsley et al., 2012).

One of the basic theories underpinning Non-Market Strategy is NIE (Doh et al., 2012). What is being picked up is that firms have to compete in an environment that is characterized by North's (1990) rules of the game. All the theories and applications about competitive strategy still apply, yet this plays out within the confines of legislation and government policy. In terms of Williamson's (2000) levels of analysis, firms are competing with each other at level 3 while being constrained by the formal rules of level 2. Some have taken up Williamson's suggestion to strategically position a firm's activities between market and hierarchy based on the transaction costs it faces. More concrete, this is about deciding whether to internalize activities, to go into partnerships of some sort, or to rely on the market (Dorobantu et al., 2017), that is, Williamsons (2000) 2nd-order and 3rd-order economizing. Others focus on corporate political activity and investigate how firms can make regulation and government policies as institutions more efficient so that fewer transaction costs have to be endured (Boddewyn & Doh, 2011; Henisz & Zelner, 2012). To Williamson (2000), this would be firms at level 3 contributing to 1st-order economizing by providing feedback to government who set the formal rules at level 2. Interestingly, Non-Market Strategy appears to leave the informal rules of level 1 alone.

Researchers who identify with the Non-Market Strategy research stream have also looked into how firms originating from one country can deal with the different institutional arrangements they will come across when operating in another country (Boddewyn & Doh, 2011; Henisz & Delios, 2004). With this, we move into the realm of IB/IS which also utilize NIE as one of the basic underpinning theoretical approaches (Hotho & Pedersen, 2012).

Like Non-Market Strategy, IB/S research has recognized that different countries have different institutional arrangements that pose different levels of transaction costs. The obvious conclusion then is that firms must take these into account when they are internationalizing. Researchers like Peng and Meyer take North's (1990) explanation of the prosperity of a country depending on the quality of the institutions in that country to the level of firms. Whether and how to enter a country is then seen to depend on what institutions are in existence and how much transaction costs these add to the activities a firm wants to engage in. Peng and Meyer concentrated first on what they label as transition economies: Eastern European countries who had to re-organize their societies after the fall of communism (Meyer, 2001; Meyer & Peng, 2005; Peng, 2003; Peng & Heath, 1996). They then moved to mostly Asian emerging economies as being less developed or differently developed, and made the same argument (Meyer et al., 2009; Peng et al., 2008).

This strand of IB/S research arrived at the same conclusion as Non-Market Strategy in that the institutional environment exists adjacent to the competitive environment (Peng, 2006; Peng et al., 2008). The focus tends to be on the specific problems of entry mode, on how to operate in a foreign country, and whether to go for a trade arrangement, some kind of joint venture with a local partner, or a wholly owned subsidiary (Domínguez et al., in press; Meyer, 2001; Pajunen, 2008; Peng, 2003; Peng & Heath, 1996). Again, it all should be aimed at minimizing transaction costs or 2nd-order economizing (Williamson, 2000), which in turn depends on how institutions have developed in a country. The less developed a country is, the more informal and market-based the entry mode should be, while countries with more developed institutions require more hierarchy by way of a wholly or partly owned subsidiary and direct investment (cf. Williamson, 2000).

With NIE and its applications in Non-Market Strategy and IB/IS, both strategic choice and implementation are taken as squarely within the agency of a strategist. A strategist is presumed to be free and able to formulate and execute a strategy. An organization is assumed to have the agency to position itself on the continuum between market and hierarchy by adopting the governance arrangements of its choice. In that sense, NIE strategizing is clearly agentic. It supposes that strategists and organizations can take initiatives and have control over their actions and outcomes. Both are taken to be autonomous, capable (albeit with cognitive limitations), and independent actors, who will behave purposefully to efficiently generate organizational outcomes.

3 Organizations as Institutions: Old Institutionalism

Old Institutionalism only got its label because New Institutionalism needed something to criticize to set out its own stall (DiMaggio & Powell, 1991). New

Institutionalism will be introduced later and is not to be confused with the New Institutional Economics (NIE) from the previous chapter. Old Institutionalism is one of several institutional theories rooted in sociology, with Philip Selznick (1949, 1957) often put at the heart of and seen as exemplary of this variant. Just like NIE, Old Institutionalism as a research project is a reaction to a dominant approach but on this occasion in organization theory. Like NIE rallying against neo-classical economics, Selznick was arguing against the then dominant conceptualization of the organization as a bureaucracy; as a collection of procedures, functions, and roles to achieve a specific goal as if it is a mechanism that can be engineered and fine-tuned to deliver a pre-defined set of outcomes as efficiently as possible. His study of the Tennessee Valley Authority (TVA) showed him that this organization did not comply with this ideal, yet the TVA was not deemed dysfunctional (Selznick, 1949). The TVA was a 1933 initiative of the Roosevelt administration to economically develop the Tennessee River basin. Selznick found the TVA as an organization adapting its purpose and understanding of itself as it developed, mostly because it was focusing on specific stakeholders. This made it move away from its original purpose; making it difficult to understand this organization as a bureaucracy and as an efficient device to achieve specific pre-defined goals.

Selznick's (1957) book *Leadership in Administration* was an attempt to understand what was going on. In it he proposes an institutional theory that recognizes there is more to an organization than it being a bureaucracy designed to achieve a specific end in the most efficient and effective manner. Like NIE questioning the assumption of rational choice in economics, Selznick questioned the means-ends assumption of rationality in organization theory. His institutional theory distinguishes between organizations as bureaucracies and organizations as institutions. To him, many organizations exist and can be understood and managed as a bureaucracy. However, some organizations develop into an institution. Some organizations institutionalize: 'to institutionalize is to infuse with value' (Selznick, 1957: 17).

The word 'value' here appears to denote something like 'meaning' in that the organization's significance to those who are involved with it exceeds it just being a means to a specific end. The organization in a way has become an end itself. Selznick likes to refer to this as fulfilling 'the expendability test'. An organization has become an institution if people care enough to want it to continue despite it having outlived its original purpose. The TVA started as a bureaucracy but became an institution because it became meaningful to a specific community for which it then became an end by itself. As the community changed the TVA adapted. More particularly, the TVA adopted environmental protection and the plight of poor African Americans and farm tenants as an important part of its remit. An organization's identification with a community 'involves the taking on of values, ways of acting and believing that are deemed important for their own sake' by this community and therefore by the organization (Selznick, 1957: 21).

Selznick writes about legitimacy – without using the word as such – as being super-imposed on and possibly replacing efficiency as the criterion by which an organization's existence should be explained at least for an organization that has become an institution. His institutional theory, which is core to Old Institutionalism, is a theory that explains whether and why an organization takes on the form of a bureaucracy or of an institution. An organization develops from a bureaucracy into an institution or institutionalizes when it becomes meaningful for and in a specific community. Selznick's institutional theory points at legitimacy as an important factor for understanding organizations.

Selznick (1957) goes on to argue that when an organization has developed into an institution, it requires leadership rather than management. Management to Selznick is technocratic and about designing and running a bureaucracy. In contrast, leadership is about developing, maintaining, but also changing when required, the meaning of the organization in relation to the community it serves. On the one hand, this is a take on running an organization that was echoed later in the literature on transformational leadership (e.g. Bass, 1991; Bennis & Nanus, 1985) where a charismatic leader is urged to take charge by formulating and propagating meaning for the organization's members. On the other hand, Selznick describes the process by which an organizations pursues its relevance for a community and also the choice of community to which it aligns itself as a negotiation and as a process characterized by organizational politics (cf. Narayanan & Fahey, 1982; Pfeffer, 1981).

Selznick (1957) also adopted the notion of 'mission' to refer to the reason why an organization as institution exists. He derived this from the military use of the term where mission is used to express the purpose of a specific military operation. He referred to the capability of an organization as institution to deliver on its mission as 'distinctive competence', which has been put forward as an early expression of the Resource-based View's core capability concept (Foss, 1997; Mahoney & Pandian, 1992), although Selznick did not associate distinctive competence with competitive advantage. Mission as the expression of an organization's purpose (Campbell, 1987), however, has become a staple term in almost every strategic management textbook.

Apart from Old Institutionalism and the work of Selznick (1949, 1957) being positioned as a stepping off point for New Institutionalism (DiMaggio & Powell, 1991), it saw application in International Business/Strategy (IB/S) by Kostova (1999; Kostova & Roth, 2002). She problematizes multinational corporations (MNCs) as having each subsidiary organized differently because each subsidiary adapted to the values and ways of acting and thinking that are characteristic of the country in which it operates. These differences then explain why the adoption of headquarter designed and prescribed universal practices and procedures among all subsidiaries in an unequivocal manner is so difficult if not impossible. The argumentation subsequently was extended by seeing it as essential for local subsidiaries of MNCs to adapt to what is considered legitimate in the countries they operate in, explicitly criticizing the 'isomorphism' thesis (that will be explained later) of New Institutionalism (Kostova & Zaheer, 1999; Kostova et al., 2008).

Applying Old Intuitionalism in the realm of strategic management further, recognizing that organizations as an institution are 'infused with value', and as being meaningful for internal and external stakeholders rather than just being a 'tool' for achieving pre-defined goals, the environmental survival process is about being legitimate for the community the organization serves (see Figure 3). That is a legitimacy that is mostly about providing meaning for stakeholders. Meaning is what animates the process. Which community to pick happens by way of negotiation and consequently strategists are negotiators. Selznick (1957) also recognizes that strategists have to provide meaning by formulating the organization's mission as reflecting the values of the community the organization associates with. By implication, the organizational strategy process is a combination of organizational politics (Narayanan & Fahey, 1982) and management of meaning (Smircich & Morgan, 1982).

The underlying process principles, by Selznick's (1996) own admission as with NIE, are derived from Methodological Individualism. The institutionalization of an

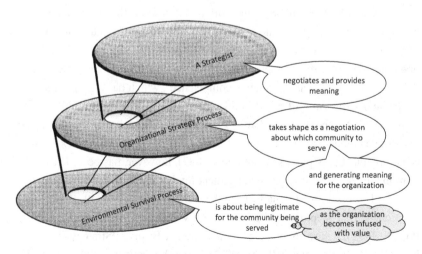

Figure 3 Old institutionalism strategizing.

organization by infusing it with value is taken to be the consequence of the actions and choices of organization members, although Selznick does recognize this happens through negotiation and compromise rather than by design. For this reason, there is some ambivalence about a strategist's agency. On the one hand, Selznick (1957) appears to propagate a form of leadership with a strategist taking charge of providing meaning for the organization, much like what was later proposed as transformational leadership (Bass, 1991; Bennis & Nanus, 1985). Selznick's use of the word 'mission' chimes with this as well, preceding its later popularity for expressing an organization's purpose (Campbell, 1987). On the other hand, which constituents the organization associates with or, in other words, for whom the organization is meaningful and what this meaning is about, develops by way of negotiation, downplaying the possibility of a strategist or leader taking charge. Kostova (1999; Kostova & Roth, 2002; Kostova & Zaheer, 1999; Kostova et al., 2008) puts a finer point on this by investigating and confirming how difficult it is for MNCs to manage different legitimacy requirements across various countries. Apparently, you cannot provide meaning by decree.

4 Organizations and Isomorphism: New Institutionalism

Up to the 1970s, the idea of organizations having to have a formal structure was not questioned as such. If organization structure was problematized, it was by enquiring how you could best translate the organization's purpose or reason for its existence into an organizational design of departments, functions, job descriptions, procedures, and layers of management. Old Institutionalism originating with Selznick (1949, 1957) contrasting organizations that are designed and structured in pursuit of rationally and of efficiently getting a job done with organizations that are infused with value to the extent that rationality and efficiency became less important. Selznick branded organizations infused with value as institutions.

Meyer and Rowan (1977) and Tolbert and Zucker (1983) went another route in questioning whether organizations are just means to an end. They started wondering about this because it became commonly recognized that for organizations to be effective, these had to rely more on the informal organization than on how an organization formally had been structured. 'Doing everything by the book' is a sure way of tripping an organization up. To answer this conundrum, they in a way extended the 'infused with value' argument by claiming that rationality and efficiency are also values. This means that an organization having a formal structure in pursuit of rationality and efficiency is a norm to which every organization must submit to be considered legitimate. Having a formal structure then is more of a symbol to signal that the organization is legitimate instead of formal structure contributing to the organization being efficient and effective.

Meyer and Rowan (1977) and Tolbert and Zucker (1983) with DiMaggio and Powell (1983) took the argument one step further by not only claiming that organizations have a formal structure to remain legitimate rather than efficient; often sticking with organizational designs long beyond these having been effective and rational if these ever were, but also that organizations are iso-morphic. Organizations all appear the same because organizations have to conform to the same norms and values. It are the norms and values as these exist outside the organization, which are referred to as institutions in what was labelled as New Institutionalism (Powell & DiMaggio, 1991). Even the idea of organization itself as a means to get something done was put forward as having been institutionalized as a norm (Zucker, 1983).

The process principles that underpin this line of thought moved away from the Methodological Individualism of New Institutional Economics and Old Institutionalism. Instead of institutions either as constraints or as organizations infused with value appearing as an effect that can be reasoned back to some form of deliberate choice by individual actors, New Institutionalism assumed institutions as having been socially constructed (Berger & Luckmann, 1966).

Social construction is presented as a collective endeavour involving several, if not many, people. It is a process that still acknowledges that people make choices but also sees an effect of extra-human arrangements that are referred to as social constructions to which people must conform. Berger and Luckmann (1966) present these social constructions as emerging by way of the three steps of habitualization, externalization, and socialization. Habitualization occurs when people develop ways of dealing with situations or problems to then deploy the same solution every time a specific situation occurs or as a particular problem arises. At some point, this solution becomes the norm for dealing with the problem, with such a norm taking on an existence outside or externally from the people who deploy solutions to situations. In this way norms and values of how you should interpret a situation and of how you should behave in this situation become institutionalized as a social construction. People who might not be familiar with the norms and values can then be socialized into them so that they know how to behave and how to think.

Berger and Luckmann (1966) provided their Social Construction theory to explain how social order in society emerges. Meyer and Rowan (1977), Tolbert and Zucker (1983), and DiMaggio and Powell (1983) took this sociological theory to explain how and why organizations are isomorphic, predominantly by stating that institutions are social constructions. Further research in the realm of New Institutionalism quickly moved beyond the norm of organizations having to have a formal structure and the values of having to be rational and efficient, to apply the requirement of legitimacy and its effect on organizations more generally to many other norms and values that are present. The thesis is that organizations strive to be legitimate to justify their existence and to avoid being sanctioned and starved from the resources they need to function. It is perhaps this thesis of isomorphism that is the main distinction between Old Institutionalism and New Institutionalism, with old institutionalism providing an explanation of why organizations (as institutions themselves) are all unique, as they identify with their respective communities, while new institutionalism purports that all organizations are the same, as they all conform to the same institutionalized expectations.

Indeed, to some New Institutionalism is just about isomorphism (Glynn & D'Aunno, 2023; Ocasio & Gai, 2020). Isomorphic effects have been observed, for instance, with the adoption of certain technologies (Robertson et al., 1996), entering strategic alliances (Garcia-Pont & Nohria, 2002), or adopting ISO 9000 standards (Guler et al., 2002). Organizations were found to take these on not because of their inherent qualities or usefulness, but because adopting a particular technology, entering strategic alliances, or becoming ISO certified had become the norm and therefore everybody did this.

To others it developed into being about organizations remaining legitimate by conforming to norms and values exogenous to them (Jepperson, 1991; Scott, 2014). More generally, the organizational field became the locus of the institutionalized norms and values that prescribe how organizations are expected to behave (Zietsma et al., 2017). An organizational field is defined by DiMaggio and Powell (1983: 148) as 'those organizations that, in the aggregate, constitute a recognized area of institutional life: key suppliers, resource and product consumers, regulatory agencies, and other organizations that produce similar services or products'.

This inspired research that linked the activities and success of organizations to institutionalized expectations that exist at field level. For instance, Leblebici et al.(1991) took US radio broadcasting as an organizational field to find that over time, it was institutionalized differently. Initially radio broadcasting was about manufacturing radio sets, then about listening to national radio networks, to become about listening to local radio stations, with each era providing a different way in which you could make a profit from radio broadcasting. Hargadon and Douglas (2001) explained that Edison's innovation of the electric light bulb had been successful because the way in which he set himself up as a business of providing illumination mimicked how illumination was provided already by way of gas lighting technology. Such observations and explanations led to suggestions that firm success and survival are not just a matter of competitive advantage but also a matter of compliance to institutionalized expectations to the extent that the way in which competition occurs and what defines competitive advantage is also a consequence of these institutionalized expectations (DiMaggio & Powell, 1991; Lawrence, 1999).

Some ambiguity crept in about what exactly an 'institution' is and in its wake how we are to understand legitimacy. One of the discrepancies is whether an institution is something cognitive or something social. When an institution is seen as cognitive, it is taken as an attribute of an individual person and as residing in somebody's mind, albeit with large numbers of people sharing the same thoughts to qualify as an institution. An institution as a cognitive phenomenon then is an idea or a thought and is likened to 'schemata' and 'frames' or thinking modes as developed in cognitive psychology. For instance, from a cognitive point of view an institution like 'primary school' is a thinking frame in people's minds by which they attach meaning to a building by recognizing it as a school as well as providing an understanding of the activities that happen inside. When an institution is seen as social, it is taken as having an existence outside and independently from human perception. An institution as a social phenomenon has a largely intangible, but real, presence as a norm or a value despite of how individual people think about it, albeit can manifest itself in tangible ways. From a social point of view, 'primary school' as an institution is the norm by which children of a certain age are educated as opposed to home schooling or to not being educated at all, which exists whether you agree with it or not; even when you as an individual do not understand the idea of education whatsoever. The school building and how it is laid out is the tangible manifestation of primary education and how it is supposed to be done.

Another discrepancy is about whether an institution is only an institution when it is in some way formalized as a rule or a form of regulation or whether institutions exist largely in informal ways with some of them formalized into rules and regulations. From a formal regulation point of view primary education and primary schools are an institution because legislation obliges people to send their children to school from a certain age onwards. From an informal point of view, the primary school is a formalized form of the norm of having children educated alongside more informal arrangements like home schooling.

These discrepancies also translate into different understandings of legitimacy. Cognitive legitimacy then refers to how well an organization fits with common thought patterns or shared ideas. Normative legitimacy is about conforming to social norms and values. Regulative legitimacy is about how well an organization abides by the formal rules and regulations that apply to it. Scott (2014) attempts to synthesize all three approaches by referring to the regulative, normative, and cognitive as the three pillars of institutions. He defines institutions as 'consist[ing] of cognitive, normative, and regulative structures and activities that provide stability and meaning to social behavior.

Institutions are transported by various carriers – cultures, structures, and routines – and they operate at multiple levels of jurisdiction' (Scott, 2014: 33). Scott's three pillars have been popular in research on institutions and their effects even beyond the realm of New Institutionalism (Boddewyn & Doh, 2011; Glynn & D'Aunno, 2023; Hoffman, 1999; Kostova, 1999; Oliver, 1992). Nevertheless, declaring the cognitive, normative, and regulative as aspects of an institution ignores the somewhat fundamental differences that exist between each of these different understandings of what an institution is.

With his definition of what an institution is Scott (2014) also extends the original focus of New Institutionalism away from organizational fields as the source and benchmark of what is legitimate and where institutions reside as per DiMaggio and Powell (1983). Institutions to him can be rooted in at least six different levels. These are the levels of the world system, the societal level, the organizational field, the organizational population, the organization, and the organizational subsystem. Rather than just the organizational field, to Scott organizations must abide with institutionalized expectations originating from at least six different sources.

The more general New Institutionalism requirement that organizations and firms in particular have to be legitimate by conforming to institutionalized norms, values, and ideas made Oliver (1991) propose that organizations have five ways to strategically respond. The options are acquiesce, compromise, avoidance, defiance, or manipulation. 'Acquiesce' means that the organization accepts the norms, values, and ideas for what these are and conforms to them. If we take the primary school example again, norms, values, and ideas manifest themselves in what it is that is to be taught, and in some countries, this developed into a national curriculum. Acquiesce means that a school unquestionably adopts this. This will also lead to isomorphism among all organizations that choose this option. Oliver recognizes that there are occasions that some institutionalized requirements are at odds with each other. For instance, with contentious subjects in a curriculum when nationally agreed ways of teaching certain elements are at odds with local sentiments and convictions. In those situations, an organization can opt to 'compromise'. A school can teach both what is nationally required and what is locally preferred. Organizations can also opt to conceal not conforming to (some) institutionalized expectations. That happens when a school decides to deviate from the national curriculum but does not officially acknowledge this. That is the 'avoid' option. 'Defiance' as an option means that the organization openly resists conforming to what is expected. This happens when a school deviates and openly acknowledges that it is doing this. 'Manipulation' means that the organization actively tries to change (some) institutionalized norms, values, and ideas. A school might become active in a social movement to change the national curriculum.

There is a whole range of considerations that organizations are expected to take into account when choosing for either one of these options, roughly depending on how it understands its interests and how much scope there is to follow an option through. Oliver (1991, 1997a, 1997b) sees legitimacy as separate from competitive advantage, or as she prefers it, the institutional environment and the task environment. When the organization identifies more with the demands from the task environment and the demands from the institutional environment are getting in the way, organizations would see their interests in terms of competitive advantage rather than legitimacy and will go against what the institutional environment tells them to do.

Looking at the various ways in which the notion of institution is understood in New Institutionalism it can be easily recognized that Non-Market Strategy as an area of research within strategic management is pre-occupied mostly with institution as formal rule or regulation and with regulative legitimacy; all at the level of a country because a country is taken as the primary legislative entity. This is especially the case because Non-Market Strategy is seen as adjacent to and separate from competitive strategy and as being about corporate political activity aiming to affect legislation from impeding a firm's competitive advantage, if not enhancing it (Baron, 1995a, 1995b; de Figueirdo, 2009; Hillman & Hitt, 1999; Holburn & Vanden Bergh, 2008). There have been calls to extend the notion of institution within Non-Market Strategy to include cognitive and normative legitimacy but that has remained rather underdeveloped (Doh et al., 2012; Henisz & Zelner, 2012; Mellahi et al., 2016).

A similar focus on regulative legitimacy is present in IB/S research, with a call for extending how the notion of institution is conceptualized having been made as well (Hotho & Pedersen, 2012). That is apart from the work done by Richard Whitley (1992, 1999, 2007) who developed almost singlehandedly the Business Systems approach in IB/S. He took the basic New Institutionalism idea that every firm has to comply with existing institutionalized expectations to argue that these expectations are different for different parts of the world (Whitley, 1990, 1994). Consequently, and drawing on the isomorphism argument, the way business is done will be the same within a country but vary between them. In Whitley (1991, 1994) the idea of country specific institutionalized patterns of doing business is developed into the notion of 'business system'. A business system is characterized by institutionalized norms, values, and ideas about how people in organizations are managed and controlled, how governance and ownership play their part, and how exchange relationships between firms are configured. With these three aspects, he found striking differences between how this was arranged in Japan, Korea, and Taiwan/ Hong Kong and by implication with the USA and the UK. The differences between each business system were traced back to a country's historical development as a distinct society.

More specifically, in the USA and the UK managers are expected to control firms with formal structures and systems, with ownership and shareholding being emphasized for creating conglomerates, while relying on impersonal market exchange to trade goods and services between firms and with customers. Whitley (1991) found that Japan's business system centres on the *keiretsu*: an informal business group in which loyalty plays a large part rather than formal structure, ownership, and impersonal economic exchange. Korea's business system is characterized by the *cheabol*: a diversified conglomerate run and controlled by a single person or family, while Taiwan/Hong Kong's business system is organized around family firms and kinship relations. In a way, Whitley took Scott's (2014) societal and organizational field levels and brought them to bear upon the organization level for the countries that he investigated.

All this allows him to make several points that are relevant for strategic management. Most importantly, he concludes that every firm has to function within a business system. This means that rather than seeing legitimacy as a requirement adjacent to competitive advantage – as is done by Oliver (1991, 1997a, 1997b), in Non-Market Strategy, and up to this point in IB/IS – the norms, values, and ideas that come with a business system define how a firm has to operate in a country. In short and agreeing with DiMaggio and Powell (1991) and Lawrence (1999), legitimacy tells firms how to compete because all business and economic activity is institutionally embedded. Therefore, differences between business systems explain differences in innovation patterns and strategies on a country-by-country basis, while firms act largely isomorphic – that is variations on a theme – within a country (Whitley, 2000).

Whitley also argues against the assumption of increasing globalization based on what to him is a misconception of there being universally applicable insights and 'best practice' ways of working. At best this is the spread of the Anglo-Saxon business system prevalent in the USA and the UK to other parts of the world, yet with alternative business systems in other countries not necessarily being converted (Whitley, 1998, 2003). He also reckons that multinational corporations who manage to be successful across different business systems develop an advantage specific to them of dealing with different institutionalized requirements compared to exclusively domestic firms (Whitley, 2007).

New Institutionalism set out to explain why organizations behave in the way that they do. The explanation put forward is about having to remain legitimate by conforming to norms, values and ideas as institutionalized arrangements that have developed external to the organization. Regarding the relevance of New Institutionalism for strategic management, for the environmental survival process, the requirement to remain legitimate, as with Old Institutionalism, has been clearly stated. On this occasion, rather than the organization becoming an institution because it has become infused with value (Selznick, 1957), institutions primarily appear external to the organization as institutionalized arrangements of norms, values, and ideas by which an organization is expected to abide. This has been elaborated as specific as the norm of being effective and rational (Meyer & Rowan, 1977), and more general as a configuration of expectations and requirements, which takes on the form of a business system (Whitley, 1999), or as an almost all-encompassing world system within which five more specific levels reside (Scott, 2014). Interestingly, if competitive advantage is about being different (Porter, 1996), conforming to institutional pressures and isomorphism is about being the same.

However, some ambiguity about what exactly an institution is crept in. The first issue is about how an institution exists. Is an institution a cognitive phenomenon residing in people's minds as a cognitive scheme or framework albeit shared among many? Or is an institution a social phenomenon existing independently from how people think about it; as having a real but intangible presence, albeit sometimes manifested in tangible ways. The second issue is about whether and when something is institutionalized. Is the term of 'institution' reserved for formal rules and legislation and do we only take formal regulation into account when we explain why an organization behaves in the way that it does? Or are all norms, values, and ideas that might be present referred to as institutions, the formal and the informal, the clear and the not-so-clear? Can you simply ignore these issues and like Scott (2014) declare the cognitive, the social, and the regulative as the three pillars of an institution?

A third issue is about whether institutions occupy a realm or institutional environment that is separate from the resource and competitive constrictions put upon organizations and firms. The latter has been either referred to as the task environment (Oliver, 1991) or the market environment (Doh et al., 2012). Or whether everything in the environment is institutionally embedded? This position assumes that the way in which resources are distributed and become available, and the way competition takes place, is all dictated by institutionalized norms, values, and ideas. Both assumptions are present within New Institutionalism, and they are mutually exclusive.

The process principles underpinning New Institutionalism are mostly derived from Berger and Luckmann (1966) with institutions taken as coming into existence by way of social construction. When it comes to making this relevant for strategic management there is a parting of ways. Going in one direction, institutional pressures and the requirement of legitimacy is separated from competitive pressures and the requirement of competitive advantage. Going in the other direction, socially constructed institutional arrangements are seen as structuring how competition takes place.

Oliver's (1991) distinction between institutional environment and task environment is indicative for going in the first direction. It separates being legitimate from being competitive. Researchers in Non-Market Strategy appear to argue that competitiveness always trumps legitimacy (Baron, 1995a, 1995b; de Figueirdo, 2009; Hillman & Hitt, 1999; Holburn & Vanden Bergh, 2008). The environmental survival process for the non-market part of strategy then is about how to protect the firm from legislative interference that impedes its competitiveness, and possibly lobby for government action that enhances competitiveness (see Figure 4). The notion of legitimacy is restricted to adhering to formal rules and legislation. To execute Non-Market Strategy, firms are told to engage in corporate political activity. It very much fits with the textbook notion of strategic management as planning for competitive positioning to then also take the non-market environment into account. Like textbook strategic management, the process is animated by competitiveness.

The alternative direction for strategic management that applies New Institutionalism is to suppose that the way in which competition is structured is a consequence of a socially constructed institutionalized arrangement. This argument is found in Whitley's (1999) concept of business systems. In the strategic management literature, the argument is also present in concepts like cognitive communities (Huff, 1982; Porac et al., 1989) and industry recipes (Spender, 1989) that denote that executives who manage companies that are in

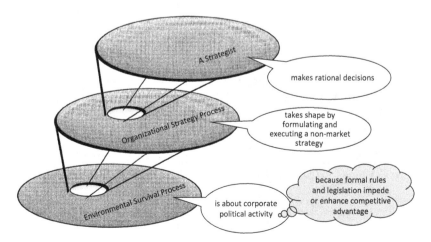

Figure 4 New institutionalism strategizing as per non-market strategy.

the same line of business, by way of how they have firms operate and compete, socially construct an industry structure or a market segmentation, which in turn informs how they understand their environment.

The environmental survival process then is about complying with institutionalized expectations as these are pressing down on the organization, and resulting in isomorphism (see Figure 5). The organizational strategy process reflects – and is informed by how well executives are socialized in – the institutionalized arrangements as these exist in the environment. There might well be a strategic planning process in place, but this largely serves the function of abiding by institutionalized arrangements, especially because it is the norm to plan when you do strategy. Because it makes sense that if you want to be in a certain line of business, you operate in the way that these businesses are expected to operate. If you would not conform, customers, suppliers, personnel, anybody, would not understand what your business is about and would therefore not engage with you. Consequently, the process is animated by compliance.

The isomorphism thesis in New Institutionalism questions the notion of strategic choice. A strategist essentially is a conformist who agrees with what is being expected. With the task or market environment seen as embedded within an institutional environment, carving out the possibility of strategic agency becomes problematic because all activity results from what institutions prescribe people to do (Beckert, 1999; Holm, 1995). Despite social construction (Berger & Luckmann, 1966) being phenomenological and therefore leaning towards the agentic side of the spectrum, its application here emphasizes the externalization aspect. An institution is mostly taken as prescribing how people are supposed to behave. However, by seeing competitiveness and legitimacy as

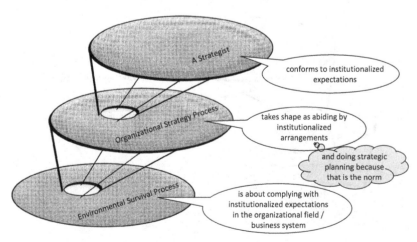

Figure 5 New institutionalism strategizing.

separate demands put upon an organization, Non-Market Strategy has circumvented this rather deterministic quality of New Intuitionalism. Because legitimacy is taken as subordinate to competitiveness, the assumption of strategic choice is restored. The textbook form of strategizing remains intact with strategists and organizations free to choose their competitive strategy to treat institutions – understood as formal rules and legislation – as subjected to their corporate political activity.

5 Explaining Institutions: Institutionalization and Institutional Entrepreneurship as Episodic Change

If New Institutionalism is about the presence of institutions explaining what organizations and people do, then institutionalization is about explaining the presence of institutions and how these have taken shape to have this effect on organizations and people. DiMaggio (1988) came up with the notion of institutional entrepreneurship. He suggested that institutions 'arise when organized actors with sufficient resources (institutional entrepreneurs) see in them an opportunity to realize an interest that they value highly' (14). He expects that this will involve a highly politicized process because anyone who has an interest in preserving the existing institutionalized arrangements will put up a fight. There have been many case studies of institutional change that indeed report on there being a struggle. Furthermore, a large proportion of these case studies identify a particular actor as the institutional entrepreneur. Some of these case studies even provide indications as to what it takes to be a successful institutional entrepreneur. This would fill the void left by New Institutionalism as to how to understand the strategic agency by which organizations can create institutionalized arrangements that are amenable to them, and possibly what a strategist can do to make this happen.

In these case studies of institutional change and institutional entrepreneurship, the emphasis on what an institution is, moves away somewhat from the norms, values, and ideas that prescribe what activities are legitimate towards the activities themselves as these happen to be legitimized by norms, values, and ideas. Activities that have been investigated and found to be institutionalized – that is to have become taken-for-granted, regular and customary ways of doing things as a consequence of a process of institutional change – include the different ways in which firms made money in the US radio broadcasting industry (Leblebici et al., 1991), mandated sales in Norwegian fisheries (Holm, 1995), caesarean births in US hospitals (Goodrick & Salancik, 1996), nineteenth-century thrift plans in the USA (Haveman & Rao, 1997), environmentalism in the US chemical industry (Hoffman, 1999, 2001), forensic accounting in Canada (Lawrence, 1999), electric lighting replacing gas lighting (Hargadon & Douglas, 2001), recycling by US universities (Lounsbury, 2001), the Java programming language (Garud et al., 2002), the multidisciplinary practice among accountancy firms in Canada (Greenwood & Suddaby, 2006; Greenwood et al., 2002), whale watching as a business (Lawrence & Phillips, 2004), HIV/AIDS treatment advocacy in Canada (Maguire et al., 2004), product categorization and diversification in the American mutual fund industry (Lounsbury & Leblebici, 2004; Lounsbury & Rao, 2004), the popularization of photography by Kodak (Munir & Phillips, 2005), the digitization of photography (Munir, 2005), nurse practitioners in Alberta (Reay et al., 2006), the Indian modern art market (Khaire & Wadhwani, 2010), and sharing economy platforms in China (Li & Schoenherr, 2023). This is not an exclusive list but gives a flavour of the wide range of activities that can be thought of as being subjected to institutionalization. These activities having been institutionalized not only means that these are done in a particular way, but also that these are done at all. The examples all involve organizations whose existence and success depends on how they deal with their respective institutionalized arrangements, if not having had a hand in how the institutionalized arrangement took shape.

The locus of where the institutionalization and institutional change happens in these case studies is the organizational field, made up of those organizations and actors who regularly interact with each other (DiMaggio & Powell, 1983). However, Hoffman (1999) proposed and worked with an alternative field definition based on organizations and actors having an interest in a particular issue. As a consequence, issue field and exchange field became alternative conceptualizations of the organizational field (Zietsma et al., 2017).

To be able to explain institutional change as being the consequence of institutional entrepreneurship, researchers had to deal with what Seo and Creed (2002) dubbed as the 'paradox of embedded agency'. This paradox became the dominant issue in research on institutional change and a persistent conceptual problem for institutional theory (Barley & Tolbert, 1997; Battilana et al., 2009; Beckert, 1999; Dorado, 2005; Fligstein, 1997; Greenwood & Suddaby, 2006; Hardy & Maguire, 2008; Haveman & Rao, 1997; Hoffman, 1999; Holm, 1995; Kondra & Hinings, 1998; Leblebici et al., 1991; Munir & Phillips, 2005; Smets et al., 2012; Sminia, 2011). If we accept that people's ability to act and their activities are a consequence of institutionalized arrangements that are external to them, how then can we account for the strategic agency required to put these institutionalized arrangements in place or change them? The cases studies on institutional entrepreneurship and institutional change came up with four solutions.

Battilana et al. (2009), Greenwood and Suddaby (2006), Hardy and Maguire (2008), Haveman and Rao (1997), Holm (1995), Lawrence and Phillips (2004), Leblebici et al. (1991), and Seo and Creed (2002) develop the 'imperfect institutionalization' argument as a first solution to bring agency back in. They claim that the institutionalized arrangements always will have inconsistencies and contradictions within them, with the pockets of ambiguity providing opportunities for institutional entrepreneurship to manifest itself. Some contend that these ambiguities appear within the institutionalized arrangements that characterize an organizational field. Others claim these ambiguities appear because of differences between the organizational field and larger institutionalized spheres like professions, communities, or society at large. Holm (1995) conceptualizes the multitude of spheres as a nested system, with a larger system bearing down on a system nested within it. A smaller system might see a push for change when it runs into practical difficulties when simultaneously abiding by the institutionalized pressures from the larger system and the institutionalized requirements posed by the smaller system. Overall, strategic agency that allows for institutional entrepreneurship is brought in by assuming that contradictions within the institutionalized arrangements offer opportunities for change.

Beckert (1999), Goodrick and Salancik (1996), and Kondra and Hinings (1998) came up with a second solution by presuming that people have leeway when confronted with institutionalized expectations. The norms, values, and ideas are taken as just providing guidance. People are assumed to have discretion to abide by them or not. This is effectively an argument that splits up agency and institutions and puts them into two different realms, with agency always having the upper hand. It devalues if not dismisses any explanatory power that institution might have as its effect is essentially mediated by agency and people pursuing their interests. The argument chimes with Oliver (1991) and those in Non-Market Strategy (e.g. Baron, 1995a) and IB/S (e.g. Peng, 2003) who separate out the market or resource environment from the institutional environment. The strategic agency that allows for institutional entrepreneurship is brought in by presuming that people act on their own interests despite the presence of institutionalized arrangements.

Barley and Tolbert (1997) and Lawrence and Phillips (2004) separate agency and institution out in time as a third solution. For this, they draw on a particular interpretation of structuration theory (Giddens, 1976, 1979, 1984). Giddens distinguishes between agency as a capability to act and social structure as rules and resources that enable and constrain actions. Both agency and structure are mutually implicated, as the activity that comes forth from agency reproduces or challenges the rules and resources while this activity is simultaneously facilitated by structure. This mutual implicating of agency and structure is referred to as 'structuration'. Barley and Tolbert (1997) suggest equating Giddens' social structure with institution to propose separating the enabling and constraining of agency by structure and the challenging and reproducing of structure by activity as happening sequentially in a kind of seesaw fashion. In this way, strategic agency that allows for institutional entrepreneurship is presumed to appear as events that are separated out in time from events during which institutions have their constraining and enabling effect.

As a fourth solution, Battilana et al. (2009), Greenwood et al. (2002), Hardy and Maguire (2008), Hoffman (1999, 2001), and Lawrence (1999) argue that exogenous shocks or jolts are the prime reason why institutional entrepreneurship occurs. Such incidents originate from outside the organizational field. These are claimed to have the effect of upsetting the existing institutionalized arrangements in such a way that the strategic agency of institutional entrepreneurship is required to restore order, or the upset is seized upon by people who want change.

The institutional change that happens because of institutional entrepreneurship is presented as episodic (Battilana et al., 2009; Greenwood et al., 2002; Hardy & Maguire, 2008). Periods of ordered activity is interspersed with periods of change during which a new and different institutionalized arrangement develops. Further specifications of how such a change process takes shape distinguishes between initial conditions and the activities that an institutional entrepreneur must engage in to effectuate change. There are also indications of what attributes an institutional entrepreneur must have to be able to act as an effective change agent.

The two arguments for strategic agency of exogenous shocks and imperfect institutionalization also appear as conditions for institutional entrepreneurship to occur (Battilana et al., 2009). Imperfect institutionalization is elaborated either as the degree of institutionalization with lesser institutionalized organizational fields providing more opportunity for change initiatives (Beckert, 1999; Goodrick & Salancik, 1996; Kondra & Hinings, 1998) or as latent contradictions that are ready to be exploited (Greenwood & Suddaby, 2006; Seo & Creed, 2002). Exogenous shocks or jolts can create practical problems which in turn are opportunities for change (Hardy & Maguire, 2008; Holm, 1995).

As DiMaggio (1988) already predicted, the process by which institutional entrepreneurship plays out is highly political with proponents of change clashing with those who want to preserve the existing institutionalized arrangements (Beckert, 1999; Fligstein, 1997, 2001; Garud et al., 2002; Hoffman, 1999, 2001; Holm, 1995). The actual process is maybe best described as a war of words and as highly discursive in making contrastive claims about what is right and what is wrong; what is legitimate and what is not legitimate (Fligstein, 1997, 2001; Hardy & Maguire, 2008; Leblebici et al., 1991; Maguire et al., 2004; Munir & Phillips, 2005; Reay et al., 2006). Ideas and interpretations define what interests people have, while interests tell them what ideas and interpretations to favour (Holm, 1995). Greenwood et al. (2002: 75) introduced the notion of 'theorization' – 'the rendering of ideas into understandable and compelling formats' – as being key for how the institutionalized arrangements will take shape anew (also see Greenwood & Suddaby, 2006; Maguire et al., 2004; Munir, 2005; Suddaby & Greenwood, 2005). However, the process is seen as essentially indeterministic in that it is not clear from the outset whether a change initiative will succeed and what shape the institutionalized arrangements will be in when things have settled down again (Lawrence & Phillips, 2004). The activities that institutional entrepreneurs engage in include resource mobilization, providing rationales in favour of and against change, and developing relations and coalitions by making people understand that their interests are aligned (Battilana et al., 2009; Hardy & Maguire, 2008). Those who oppose the change initiative do the same.

An institutional entrepreneur as an actor has been endowed with various attributes. As a person, they are expected to have reflexivity (Giddens, 1984) in being able to recognize issues with existing institutionalized arrangements and to be visionaries by being able to sketch out new and better arrangements (Beckert, 1999; Garud et al., 2002; Mutch, 2007). The latter is reminiscent of Selznick's (1957) leadership in Old Institutionalism. Fligstein (1997: 398) reckons that an institutional entrepreneur must be an operator with the 'social skill' 'to motivate cooperation in other actors by providing those actors with common meanings and identities in which actions can be undertaken and justified'. Drawing on Lukes (1974), he provides a range of power play tactics that can be utilized (Fligstein, 1997, 2001).

Part of the attributes of an institutional entrepreneur is also their position in the organizational field. Their subject position – 'a socially constructed and legitimated identity available to actors in the field' (also see Hardy & Maguire, 2008; Maguire et al., 2004: 658) – can make a person more or less suitable to advocate change. Ironically, being able to become an institutional entrepreneur depends on the existing institutionalized arrangements. Often, the institutional entrepreneur is taken to be a person. However, institutional entrepreneurship has also been associated with an organization or seen as a collective endeavour (Wijen & Ansari, 2007). Regarding an organization's position in the organizational field, to some it is being located at the fringes (Holm, 1995; Luo et al., 2021), to others it is being the leader in the field (Greenwood & Suddaby, 2006; Greenwood et al., 2002; Lawrence, 1999), which makes somebody best suited to be an institutional entrepreneur.

While developing and understanding institutional entrepreneurship, researchers moved away from social construction (Berger & Luckmann, 1966) for the underlying process principles, mostly in favour of structuration theory (Giddens, 1976, 1979, 1984), with Bourdieu (1977, 1990) and

(Sewell, 1992) occasionally referred to as structuration-like alternatives. Structuration theory has a more developed conceptualization of agency than social construction. As was explained earlier, agency as an ability to act and exercise choice is mutually implicated with social structure or the institutionalized arrangements. Giddens labels this as 'the duality of structure'. Social structure is drawn upon when activity occurs, as it enables and constrains agency, and is simultaneously reproduced or challenged, as activity is happening. Instead of an institution being understood as a social construction and as bearing down on people and organizations as in New Institutionalism, in trying to get to grips with institutional entrepreneurship and change, the focus is now on institutionalization being understood and elaborated as a process of structuration within which agency has a presence, albeit enabled and constrained by structure. Furthermore, structuration and therefore institutional entrepreneurship are animated by reflexivity. Reflexivity refers to 'the monitored character of the ongoing flow of social life' (Giddens, 1984: 3). To Giddens, it is more than a cognitive ability of an individual human actor to rationalize but also to question what is going on because reflexivity also plays out socially, implicating rules, resources, and other actors as activity happens. Nevertheless, it makes that a purposeful actor can always decide to act differently.

The notion of legitimacy has been expanded to also include pragmatic legitimacy (Suchman, 1995). New Institutionalism already had normative or moral legitimacy which is about whether activity is allowed, and cognitive legitimacy which is about the definition of the situation and what is the right interpretation. Pragmatic legitimacy is about resource allocation and what people get out of the activity. If normative/moral and cognitive legitimacy references the normative and discursive rules in Giddens' (1984) social structure, pragmatic legitimacy is about resources. Similarly, any activity can be found to communicate cognitive legitimacy, sanction normative or moral legitimacy, and exercise power by using and allocating resources.

Institutionalization is the process by which institutions come about. The notion of institutional entrepreneurship was coined and developed to account for the strategic agency by which people and organizations can have a hand in how the institutionalized arrangements take shape. The individual strategist then becomes an institutional entrepreneur and a challenger of existing institutions (see Figure 6). With it, the organizational strategy process is always politically charged. If there is a formal strategic planning process in place, this is one of the many opportunities to negotiate. The strategist therefore must be understood as being a political animal, pursuing interests by negotiating about meaning, norms and values, rules, and resources.

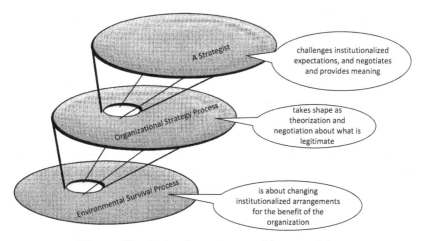

Figure 6 Institutional entrepreneurship strategizing.

The organizational survival process is about how to change institutionalized arrangements in the organizational field for the benefit the organization. Or if these arrangements happen to be beneficial already, how to prevent them from being altered. Such contestation can see high levels of ambiguity as the process plays out. The change process also is taken as largely indeterministic in that outcomes are not clear from the onset. How things eventually settle down only becomes clear in the course of time. Over time, strategists are expected to see episodes of institutional change alternated with periods of institutional stability. However, to theoretically accommodate strategic choice, a solution to the paradox of embedded agency had to be found. Four have been proposed: leeway, imperfect institutionalization, separation of agency and structure in time, and exogenous shock.

The indeterministic nature of the process puts an additional spin on the possibility of strategic choice. The strategic agency that makes institutional entrepreneurship only refers to the possibility of initiative. Despite an entrepreneur's best efforts and maybe having all the required characteristics, there is no guarantee of success. Consequently, in periods of change and ambiguity, strategy is about ploys at best (Mintzberg, 1987). It is about attempts to outmanoeuvre the opposition about what should be considered as cognitively, normatively, and pragmatically legitimate without knowing in advance whether the ploy will work. Possibly only in periods of relative stability, strategic planning and execution could work because it is reasonable to expect that the institutional continuity can be relied upon to sketch out what the future will look like, to then act accordingly, albeit always having the threat of an institutional entrepreneur upsetting things.

6 Intra-organizational Institutionalization: Convergent Incremental and Radical Strategic Change

The notion of isomorphism in New Institutionalism suggests that organizations adapt to institutionalized arrangements that exist in the organizational field and beyond to remain legitimate. Institutional change and entrepreneurship are about going against these institutionalized arrangements and are mostly problematized and investigated as happening at field level. You would expect that organizations participating in institutional entrepreneurship and change would have to organize themselves accordingly and maybe have to change themselves to be part of field-level change. Scott (2014) describes organizations and organizational sub-units as levels below the field where institutionalized arrangements and therefore institutionalization also appear. However, how to understand intra-organizational institutionalization has received relatively little attention (Smets et al., 2012). This is apart from Old Institutionalism where Selznick (1957) supposes that all organizations that have become institutions as he defines them – that is only those organizations that have become 'infused with value' – display decision-making processes that are predominantly political in nature when these decisions are about which values to pursue.

To get to grips with institutionalization inside organizations, Greenwood and Hinings (1996) propose to combine New Institutionalism with Old Institutionalism. They arrived at this proposition in a somewhat roundabout way by questioning the concept of 'organizational structure' as it was used in contingency theory (Ranson et al., 1980) to end up developing the concept of 'design archetype' and arrive at a theory of strategic change (Greenwood & Hinings, 1988, 1993; Hinings & Greenwood, 1988a, 1988b). In doing so, they abandoned Selznick's (1957) distinction between organizations as bureaucracies and organizations as institutions by taking every organization as having been institutionalized.

Ranson et al. (1980) open a discussion whether to understand 'organization structure' as it was conceptualized within contingency theory (Blau, 1974; Woodward, 1965) as referring to formal structure. They argue that an organization's structure should be understood as centred on an organizations 'interpretative scheme'. 'Organizational structures are shaped and constituted by members' provinces of meaning, by their deep-seated interpretive schemes, and by the surface articulation of values and interests' (Ranson et al., 1980: 5). They contend that the concept of organization structure should be based on how actually people engage with each other in organizations. The resulting interaction structure is informed by how people understand their organization and their own activities within it; not on how it is designed to function. Part of their argument to emphasize the interpretative scheme for understanding organization structure is the New Institutionalism thesis that organizational-level interpretative schemes are derived from field-level institutionalized expectations (Meyer & Rowan, 1977).

Subsequently, Hinings and Greenwood (1988a, 1988b) and Greenwood and Hinings (1988, 1993) move away from contingency theory into a more configurational approach (Miles & Snow, 1978; Miller & Friesen, 1984; Mintzberg, 1979). Organization, environment, and strategy process characteristics are taken to appear in distinctive packages or configurations, yet all underpinned by a specific interpretative scheme that provides meaning. They propose the concept of 'design archetype' to recognize that 'organizations operate with a limited number of configurations of structure, strategy and environment' (Greenwood & Hinings, 1988: 294). 'The structural elements and organizational processes making up the design type are strongly underpinned by provinces of meaning and interpretive schemes which bind them together in an institutionally derived normative order' (Greenwood & Hinings, 1988: 295; citing Hinings & Greenwood, 1988b: 54). To bolster their argument, they refer to various strategic change case studies that also point at the role of meaning and interpretation in the process (Child & Smith, 1987; Johnson, 1987; Pettigrew, 1985; Whipp & Clark, 1986).

Taking distinct design archetypes as the point of departure, Greenwood and Hinings (1988) hypothesize that strategic change within an organization is a movement between different archetypes and that such a transformation involves the people inside the organization changing their interpretative scheme. Furthermore, they hypothesize that these movements between archetypes will appear as four different identifiable tracks. These tracks are 'inertia' where an organization sticks to a specific archetype, 'abortion' where an organization attempts to move from one archetype to another but abandons it and moves back, 'reorientation' or 'transformation' where an organization successfully moves between archetypes, and 'unresolved excursion' where an organization ends up being stuck halfway.

Testing this they found that English Local Authorities feature two archetypes (Greenwood & Hinings, 1993; Hinings & Greenwood, 1988a).

> The heteronomous professional bureaucracy archetype conceives organizations as administrative vehicles for the delivery of essentially services [...]. In this conception, the range of a municipal government's responsibilities is a consequence of historical accident rather than of policy intent, and the domain of the local authority is the sum of its responsibilities, each treated as a separate activity. The corporate bureaucracy archetype, in contrast, emphasizes the organization as an instrument of community governance. [...] The role of the

organization is not administrative, implementing legally prescribed services, but governmental, combining packages of services and interventions in a strategic fashion. (Greenwood & Hinings, 1993: 1063–1064)

They also found that many authorities operate in a way that comes close to either template but that some are incoherent in that they display characteristics of both. Additionally, they report that observing these local authorities over time indicates that each of the four tracks of inertia, abortion, transformation, and unresolved reorientation are discernible. These patterns are also found with Canadian sports organizations, albeit with archetypes specific to this field (Kikulis et al., 1992, 1995).

This process conceptualization of combining archetypes with change tracks or trajectories is presented as bringing New Institutionalism to bear upon the institutionalization happening inside organizations (Greenwood & Hinings, 1996). Going into the detail of what happens between the people inside organizations as these organizations move along one of these change tracks, they go back to Old Institutionalism and Selznick's reporting of political behaviour in decision-making. Greenwood and Hinings (1996) propose a framework that combines exogenous factors ('market, context, institutional context) with endogenous dynamics ('interests, values, power dependencies, and capacity for action'). More specifically, they presume there are different 'interests' and 'value commitments' in an organization (cf. Selznick, 1957). Dissatisfaction with whether interests are catered for inspires attempts at change and the amount of dissatisfaction indicates a pressure for change. There are also differences in value commitments in terms of both how committed people are and how many different value commitments are present, which point at whether there will be change.

Furthermore, power dependencies and the capability for action facilitate or impede change. Power dependencies are described as 'The relations of power and domination that enable some organizational members to constitute and recreate organizational structures according to their preferences thus becomes a critical point of focus' (Greenwood & Hinings, 1996: 1038). Capability for action is described as 'having sufficient understanding of the new conceptual destination, its having the skills and competencies required to function in that new destination, and its having the ability to manage how to get to that destination' (1040).

Similar frameworks are developed by Newman (2000), Hoffman (2001), and Delmas and Toffel (2008), also referencing Selznick (1957) for the inherent political nature of intra-organizational institutionalization. Hoffman (2001) and Delmas and Toffel (2008) are interesting because they link the different interests and value expectations to the different functions within an organization and the associated departments. Zilber (2002) links the political nature of intra-organizational institutionalization to rival interpretative schemes that are local adaptations of wider held beliefs. Additionally, Kondra and Hurst (2009) suggest that the isomorphism mechanisms of coercion, mimicry, and norms (DiMaggio & Powell, 1983) operate within an organization just as much as on it. Battilana and Casciaro (2012) concentrate on the individual change agent and find that this person's network in the organization is linked with the likelihood this agent will initiate change, yet that this same network will also affect whether the initiative will be successful, depending on how much the initiative diverges from the institutionalized arrangements.

Most of this research on the politics of intra-organizational institutionaliza-tion – with the exception of Zilber (2002) – is what Van de Ven (1992) would describe as a processual variance theorizing. It treats process as a set of variables among others to hypothesize causal relationships between them, resulting in nothing more but comparative statics (Pettigrew, 1997). This kind of research theorises and on occasion tests what circumstances inside and outside the organization increase the likelihood of change happening. There is little about how this change plays out. However, the strategic change case studies that were referenced (Child & Smith, 1987; Johnson, 1987; Pettigrew, 1985; Whipp & Clark, 1986) as well as others (Grinyer et al., 1988; Quinn, 1980; Sminia, 2005; Zilber, 2002) are of a more processual nature in that these look at what is happening over time.

Quinn (1980) and Johnson (1987) find that change is realized incrementally as a sequence of compromises as and when problems occur. Like Hoffman (2001) and Delmas and Toffel (2008), Quinn (1980) links the existence of conflicting interests with the different functions and sub-units in an organiza-tion, a point also made by Prahalad and Bettis (1986) for the different businesses in diversified firms. Johnson (1987) refers to this as 'problem solving according to the paradigm', where the notion of paradigm refers to a shared interpretative scheme, 'dominant logic' (Prahalad & Bettis, 1986) or 'strategic recipe' (Child & Smith, 1987). They claim that problems are appreciated, and solutions developed through the lens of an interpretative scheme that is typical and possibly unique to an organization. Consequently, change develops incremen-tally while simultaneously confirming the plausibility of this interpretative scheme, especially when solutions appear to work.

Some managers are found to have caught on to this 'problem solving accord-ing to the paradigm' in that they deliberately play a game of confirming the interpretative scheme or undermining it to further their interests. Pettigrew (1985) labels this as 'politics as the management of meaning': 'The content of strategic change is thus ultimately a product of a legitimisation process shaped by political/cultural considerations, though often expressed in rational/analytical terms' (443). Those who comprehend the organization as being understood in terms of an interpretative scheme use opportunities inherent in this understanding to alter the interpretative scheme to favour their interests. Managers who recognize the interpretative scheme for what it is and what it does, and the process by which it takes shape, are the ones who tend to get the decision made in the way they want. Problems that confound the interpretative scheme and cause ambiguity are prime opportunities to challenge it (Johnson, 1987). The strategy process as a process of institutionalization is seen as layered in that it solves problems while simultaneously confirming or challenging and possibly changing the interpretative scheme (Sminia, 2005; Sminia & de Rond, 2012).

A later research stream under the Strategy-as-Practice banner, focusing more specifically on what strategists do (Jarzabkowski et al., 2007; Whittington, 2006), also developed a conceptualization of the strategy process that plays out over the interpretative scheme (Balogun & Johnson, 2005; Maitlis & Lawrence, 2003; Mantere, 2008), with some going into the detail of the language game by which strategist play the politics of meaning game (e.g. Rouleau, 2005; Samra-Fredericks, 2003; Vaara et al., 2004). The distinction made by Greenwood and Hinings (1996) between convergent change as an organization adapting to a design archetype and radical change as moving between archetypes resembles the distinction made by Johnson (1987) between incremental change and strategic change. With convergent or incremental change, the interpretative scheme of an organization remains intact. Radical or strategic change involves moving between interpretative schemes. Johnson (1987) reserves the adjective of strategic to indicate that it is about radical change that alters the organization's paradigm. Grinyer et al. (1988) even argue that strategic/radical change is an essential requirement for the turnaround of an ailing firm on the brink of bankruptcy.

By drawing on the strategic change literature and on Strategy-as-Practice, we end up with an understanding of institutionalization within organizations that is very similar to how institutional change and entrepreneurship at the level of the field is understood to take place. The process is seen as highly politicized and episodic in that periods of convergent incremental change are alternated with periods of radical strategic change (see Figure 7). We can refer to this as politics of meaning that makes use of the layered nature of the strategy process. The underlying process principles predominantly are derived from structuration theory (Giddens, 1976, 1979, 1984). Ranson et al. (1980) explicitly refers to it while many of the strategic change case studies are underpinned by structuration theory as well (Pozzebon, 2004; Sminia, 2009), as is the research stream in Strategy-as-Practice reported on here (Whittington, 2015). There is some

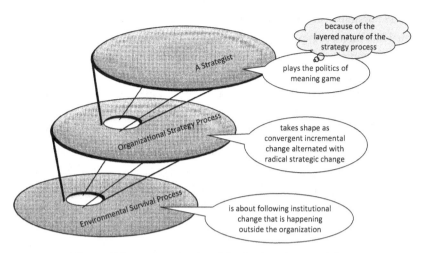

Figure 7 Intra-organizational institutional strategizing.

Strategy-as-Practice research in this realm that favoured Weick's (1995) sense-making, effectively concentrating on the rules part of the social structure at the expense of the resources part. Also similarly, intra-organizational institutional-ization is indeterministic in that the outcome only becomes clear as the process plays out. And with it being based on structuration theory, the process is animated by reflexivity (Giddens, 1984). There is some further specification in that the process is understood to be layered. And we have a clear distinction between convergent incremental change and radical strategic change. The environmental survival process has seen less elaboration here, being mostly seen as presenting institutional change that the organization must follow or be liable to becoming obsolete and fail.

Nevertheless, one of the conceptual issues that appeared with New Institutionalism appears here as well. Like the question whether an institution is essentially a cognitive phenomenon or a social phenomenon that appeared with New Institutionalism, the issue here is whether an organizational-level interpret-ative scheme is cognitive or social. Those basing themselves on structuration theory like Ranson et al. (1980) and Pettigrew (1985) see it as something social. Those basing themselves on sensemaking like Balogun and Johnson (2005), as well as Johnson (1987) earlier, elaborate it as something cognitive. Furthermore, there is the question whether an interpretive scheme is unique to an organization as the strategic change case studies seem to imply, or whether there are only a limited number of interpretive schemes that are part of organizational archetypes that are configured within an organizational field as was put forward in Greenwood and Hinings (1988) and Hinings and Greenwood (1988a).

The possibility of strategic choice is similarly problematic as with institutional entrepreneurship. There is the possibility of initiative, but the essential indeterministic nature of radical strategic change makes that the outcome is never a certainty. During periods of convergent incremental change, strategic planning might work because such change better allows for extrapolation.

7 Institutional Logics: Dealing with Institutional Complexity

The concept of institutional logics originates from Friedland and Alford (1991). This is a chapter in the book edited by Powell and DiMaggio (1991) that marks the start of the New Institutionalism variant of institutional theory. Ironically, Friedland and Alford (1991) are at odds with New Institutionalism in at least two ways. Firstly, instead of an institutional arrangement that compels an organization to be isomorphic to remain legitimate, to Friedland and Alford there are many institutional arrangements that together pose 'a potentially contradictory interinstitutional system' (240); turning the requirement to be legitimate into an impossible quest. Secondly, they presume institutional arrangements to be non-deterministic: 'no institutional order should be accorded causal primacy a priori' (240). Their argument goes against isomorphism and against a rather passive understanding of agency as conforming to institutional pressure. In effect, because of the contradictions, individual actors and organizations are presumed to be able to pick and choose which institutional arrangement they want to adhere too. It is this dealing with a range of different and often conflicting institutional logics that became the core issue that this variant of institutional theory concentrated on.

The definition of 'institutional logics' settled down with Thornton and Ocasio (2008). They define it as 'the socially constructed, historical patterns of material practices, assumptions, values, beliefs, and rules by which individuals produce and reproduce their material subsistence, organize time and space, and provide meaning to their social reality' (101). As such, it is not that different from many other definitions that try to express what an institution is. Both elements of regularity in activity and legitimization by norms, values, and ideas are present. They do make a point of distinguishing between the material and the symbolic aspects of institutional logics. The symbolic refers to the meaning that an institution provides and is linked to the norms, values, and ideas that provide legitimacy. The material refers to the non-symbolic aspect, described as 'market mechanisms [that] aggregate individual utilities and preferences, organizational competition, technology, and resource dependence' (105). The material aspect resembles what Oliver (1997a) referred to as the task environment while the symbolic aspect is similar to her institutional environment. While Oliver, Non-Market Strategy (e.g. Baron, 1995a), and IB/S (e.g. Peng, 2003) separate out the symbolic and the material and treat these as two different domains, with Institutional Logics both are seen as institutionalized. 'Key constructs in the analysis of organization, such as efficiency, rationality, participation, and values are not neutral, but are themselves shaped by the logics of the inter-institutional system' (Thornton & Ocasio, 2008: 104).

The use of 'socially constructed' does not mean that social construction theory is informing the process principals underpinning institutional logics. Berger and Luckmann (1966) are scarcely referenced. Structuration theory (Giddens, 1984) is dismissed as well as not incorporating human cognition (Thornton et al., 2012). In developing the notion of institutional logics, Friedland and Alford (1991) explicitly argue against Methodological Individualism as being over-individualized and ignoring the social. Thornton et al. (2012) develop a metatheory based on the institutional logics concept that they present as the Institutional Logics Perspective (ILP). They state their aim as offering 'a metatheoretical framework for analyzing the interrelationships among institutions, individuals, and organizations in social systems', and more specifically to provide an aid for answering 'questions of how individual and organizational actors are influenced by their situation in multiple social locations in an interinstitutional system' (2). In doing so, they – as do many authors who are identified as working with institutional logics – borrow from and combine various sociological and social psychological theoretical approaches to propose their own bespoke process principles.

Picking up on Friedland and Alford (1991), initial research utilizing institutional logics was very similar to research in institutional entrepreneurship and institutional change. These were mostly case studies of change in an institutional field, but now the change was conceptualized as moving from one institutional logic to another institutional logic. This includes Thornton and Ocasio (1999) and Thornton (2002), who describe a change of a 'logic of professions' to a 'logic of markets' in the higher education publishing industry in the USA. Gumpert (2000) analyses change in US public higher education as a moving from a logic of 'higher education as a social institution' to 'higher education as an industry'. Lounsbury (2001) and Lounsbury et al. (2003) describe the emergence of recycling as a new industry in waste management alongside disposal as the establishment of a new institutional logic next to an existing logic. Lounsbury (2002, 2007) and Lounsbury and Leblebici (2004) track changes with financial intermediaries and mutual funds in the field of finance as moving from a 'regulatory logic' to a 'market logic'. Rao et al. (2003) describe the emergence of nouvelle cuisine and it replacing classical cooking in French gastronomy as a new logic superseding an older one. Zajac and Westphal (2004) link how stock markets react differently to stock repurchase plans with a change from a 'corporate logic' to an 'agency logic' among participants in financial markets. Changes in the Alberta healthcare system are associated with a change of dominant logic from 'medical professionalism' to 'business-like health care' (Reay & Hinings, 2005). Thornton et al. (2005) relate changes in accounting, publishing, and architecture to changes regarding their respective dominant logics.

Bhappu (2000) is an example who uses the concept of institutional logic in the singular to refer to the Japanese family as an explanation for how and why Japanese corporate networks or *keiretsu* exist. She in effect makes the same point as Whitley (1991) with his notion of business system. Moorman (2002) does something similar when she proposes that consumer markets and how these operate are informed by an institutional logic specific to that market. Both these case studies of institutional change and the use of institutional logic in the singular offer little beyond similar studies based on respectively institutional change/ entrepreneurship, New Institutionalism, or inter-organizational institutionaliza-tion. These just use the term of institutional logic and its definition to denote the institutional arrangements that appear in their studies. The change process itself is also understood in very similar terms as largely discursive and requiring skilful negotiation about meaning and what is to be considered as legitimate.

Nevertheless, there appears to be one interesting statement being made with these case studies in that economics, the notion of the market mechanism, and the expectation of efficiency are just another institutional logic among many, which might gain or lose dominance (Lounsbury, 2008). The institutional logic of economics appears as a 'logic of markets' in educational publishing (Thornton, 2002; Thornton & Ocasio, 1999), a logic of 'higher education as an industry' (Gumpert, 2000), a 'market logic' with mutual funds (Lounsbury, 2002, 2007; Lounsbury & Leblebici, 2004), an 'agency logic' in corporate governance (Zajac & Westphal, 2004) and also in Lok (2010), and as a 'business-like health care' logic (Reay & Hinings, 2005). On the one hand, taking economics as just another institutional logic is a thought-provoking turn in the argument. With institutional logics, there is just one environment that is conceptualized as an interinstitutional system. By implication, this means that competitiveness is just one of many logics that organizations must deal with. On the other hand, there is a bit of a conceptual discrepancy in that economics is seen as part of the material aspect of any institutional logic while norms, values, and ideas are the symbolic aspect (Thornton & Ocasio, 2008; Thornton et al., 2012). This implies that competitiveness appears as a material aspect of an institutional logic. The issue is whether each logic has economics as part of it or is economics a particular institutional logic of its own?

Another line of research concentrates on what is more typical of the institu-tional logics variant of institutional theory: the simultaneous existence of multiple logics that are contradictory and competing with each other. This is referred to as 'institutional complexity' (Greenwood et al., 2011). It poses the question how organizations and individual actors deal with this. A range of answers has been proposed. Some suggest that a plurality of logics allows for organizations and actors to pick whatever suits them best (Binder, 2007; Coule & Patmore, 2013) to make it possible for organizations to tailor their rhetoric to the logic that somebody they have to deal with prefers (Jones & Livne-Tarandach, 2008). This is the leeway solution to the paradox of embedded agency (Seo & Creed, 2002), which was also present in institutional entrepreneurship.

Furthermore, institutional complexity is put forward as the explanation for heterogeneity, as different organizations reacting differently to the same set of institutional logics (Greenwood et al., 2011; Lounsbury, 2008; Thornton & Ocasio, 2008). Heterogeneity is the opposite of the isomorphism of New Institutionalism (DiMaggio & Powell, 1983). Others propose ways to understand how organizations manage the splits they have to perform to appear to comply with different institutional demands to remain legitimate in the eyes of the many institutional logics they are faced with (Battilana & Dorado, 2010; Kraatz & Block, 2008; Lok, 2010; Pache & Santos, 2010; Reay & Hinings, 2009).

Organizations have been observed utilizing various tactics that have subsequently been proposed as theoretical propositions of how multiple institutional logics are dealt with. Kraatz and Block (2008) offer organizations a choice between either siding with one logic and resisting other logics, compartmentalizing with different parts of the organization dealing with different logics, playing different logics against each other, or – by referring to Selznick (1957) – becoming infused with value so that the organization has its own institutional logic by which it legitimizes itself. Lok (2010) looks at people inside organizations and finds three ways in which they identify with conflicting logics by either abducting parts of a conflicting logic into a favoured logic so that it looks like they are complying, by complying with different logics in parallel, or by resisting logics in favour of other logics. Pache and Santos (2010) draw on Oliver's (1991) strategies of acquiescence, compromise, avoidance, defiance, and manipulation, but apply these to each institutional logic an organization has to contend with. Reay and Hinings (2009) found four forms of co-existence of institutional logics of separating decisions as pertaining to one logic or to another logic, of informally soliciting for opinions from one logic while adhering to the other logic, of finding another logic as a common foe, and of engaging in experimental arrangements that cater for more than one logic. Battilana and Dorado (2010: 1436) propose the concept of 'hybrid' organization: 'in the absence of institutional scripts for handling logic plurality, a new type of hybrid needs to develop a common organizational identity that enables organization members to strike a balance between logics'. Gümüsay et al. (2020b) denote this as 'elastic hybridity'. The various forms of co-existence or hybridity are the fifth solution to the paradox of embedded agency (Seo & Creed, 2002). It resembles what Brunsson (2007) has labelled as 'organized hypocrisy'.

Explaining how people and organizations deal with multiple institutional logics is at the heart of what is labelled as the Institutional Logics Perspective (ILP) (Thornton et al., 2012). This metatheory also proposes bespoke process principles for the institutional logics variant of institutional theory. It is meant to provide a framework for analysing how institutions, individuals, and organizations relate to each other so that researchers can develop explanations of how individuals and organizations are influenced by institutionalized arrangements.

Thornton et al. (2012) sees the complex constellation of many institutional logics as a multi-level phenomenon. To them the macro-societal level is an interinstitutional system consisting of cornerstone institutions or institutional orders. Examples are family, religion, state, market, profession, and corporation, but others are possible as well. Gümüsay et al. (2020a), for instance, in discussing climate change, propose the natural environment as another cornerstone institution. Each of these cornerstone institutions consists of the same building blocks, yet these have taken shape differently for each institutional order. These nine building blocks are the root metaphor; the sources of legitimacy, authority, and identity; the basis of norms, attention, and strategy; the informal control mechanisms; and the economic system. In combination, these building blocks pose an institutional logic by 'represent[ing] the cultural symbols and material practices particular to that order' (54). This interinstitutional system at times is presented as just referring to the macro-societal level but also as a multilevel complex by itself, consisting of the different layers of society, field, industry, and organization, which together pose an intricate web of connected and contradictory institutional logics.

With macro referring to society, the meso level and the micro level – as often is the case – are organizations and individuals respectively. The relationship between the macro, the meso, and the micro is elaborated based on the notion of 'microfoundations' as derived from Coleman (1990) and developed by Abell et al. (2008) and Felin and Foss (2009) by placing individuals understood in cognitive psychological terms (the microfoundations) within social phenomena. Although the macro-societal level of the interinstitutional system has many institutional logics available, at the individual level each human actor accesses only those institutional logics that come to mind, to then inform their decision-making as to how to act in a particular situation; with the choices being made activating an apparently preferred institutional logic. The organization as an intermediate or meso level appears as a filter by way of 'localized organizational practices' (Thornton et al., 2012: 92) that affects which institutional logics are available to an individual for recognition. Human activity in organizations then is analysable as the cumulative effect of institutional logics, organizational practices, and boundedly rational decision-making of individual human actors while people deal with the concrete situations that appear.

Apart from this top-down effect of the macro level through the meso level influencing the micro level, the notion of microfoundations also incorporates a bottom-up effect from the micro through the meso to the macro. The argument here is that individual human activity generated by how they cognitively recognize situations is also social activity because it involves people anticipating other people in symbolic interaction (Mead, 1934). Activity is social when individual activity becomes coordinated to generate collective effects. In a way, this deals with the ambivalence of an institution being essentially a cognitive phenomenon or essentially social, which appeared with New Institutionalism. According to Thornton et al. (2012) coordination and collective effects appear through formal organizational decision-making (Cyert & March, 1963; March & Simon, 1958; Simon, 1947), through sensemaking (Weick, 1995; Weick et al., 2005), and through mobilization (McCarthy & Zald, 1977). All three mechanisms feature communication and negotiation about 'pragmatic concerns and social cues' (Thornton et al., 2012: 95), creating a learning effect, as participants reflect on the efficacy of the social interactions. This then feeds back to the institutional logics either perpetuating or undermining them. The overall effect can be continuity or change.

Change is either deliberate or just emerging from everyday mundane activity (Thornton et al., 2012), and more of a consequence of distributed agency that happens to combine than the deliberate agency of an institutional entrepreneur. Therefore, deliberate institutional change is presented as cultural entrepreneurship (Lounsbury & Glynn, 2001) to distinguish it from institutional entrepreneurship (DiMaggio, 1988). Cultural entrepreneurship is elaborated as switching between institutional logics. It is proposed to be a process of 'vertical specialization' by moving and combining the content of building blocks across institutional orders and of 'horizontal integration' by putting building blocks together again to create a new institutional logic. It is presented as consisting of the three phases of recognizing and articulating a problem; theorizing, translating, and legitimatizing a solution; and mobilizing a community of solution advocates. It resembles institutional entrepreneurship very much in that it largely is seen as a discursive process of politics of meaning (cf. Pettigrew, 1985) yet diverges from it with the assumption that it is essentially a process of deliberate problem-solving, albeit involving many people.

Change coming out of mundane day-to-day activity is modelled on the routine dynamics approach originating from Feldman (2003) and Feldman and Pentland (2003). In routine dynamics, daily activities evolve because people adapt what they do to the variability in circumstances that they encounter. Over time, this can create a trajectory of successive incremental adjustments. Referring to Lounsbury and Crumley (2007), Thornton et al. (2012) develop this as a way to understand how 'localized organizational practices' develop and change, which by way of the feedback effects on the interinstitutional system can alter institutional logics.

As was written earlier, the institutional logics variant of institutional theory is not based on specific process principles like methodological individualism, social construction, or structuration theory. The writings eclectically draw on all of them while also rejecting them. There are many occasions where Giddens (1976, 1979, 1984) is referred to while structuration is dismissed because it is found lacking in taking human cognition into account (Thornton et al., 2012). By centring the microfoundations of institutional logics on a human's presumed ability to reflect and make decisions on what to do given the availability of various institutional logics and having to consider the situation at hand, Giddens' (1984) notion of reflexivity is somewhat present to animate the process yet understood as an individual-level cognitive faculty.

Social construction (Berger & Luckmann, 1966) hardly gets a look in while other phenomenological approaches like symbolic interactionism (Mead, 1934) and individual sensemaking (Weick, 1995) are incorporated in the microfoundations of institutional logics to provide a mechanism by which the micro level affects the meso and macro levels. Collective sensemaking is part of the organizational meso level. Despite the clear rejection of methodological individualism by Friedland and Alford (1991), it is present when institutional logics draws on behavioural theory for its elaboration of decision-making as boundedly rational (Cyert & March, 1963; March & Simon, 1958; Simon, 1947) and in how Abell et al. (2008) and Felin and Foss (2009) have developed the notion of microfoundations. There are even slight hints of actor-network theory (Latour, 2005) and Schatzki's (2002) theory of practice when Lounsbury and Crumley (2007) and Thornton et al. (2012) refer to routine dynamics (Feldman, 2003; Feldman & Pentland, 2003).

Recognizing the presence of multiple institutional logics, this variant of institutional theory mostly concentrates on how people and organizations are

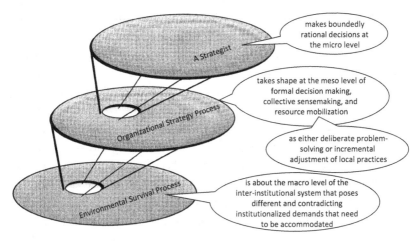

Figure within image contains:
makes boundedly rational decisions at the micro level

takes shape at the meso level of formal decision making, collective sensemaking, and resource mobilization

as either deliberate problem-solving or incremental adjustment of local practices

is about the macro level of the inter-institutional system that poses different and contradicting institutionalized demands that need to be accommodated

A Strategist

Organizational Strategy Process

Environmental Survival Process

Figure 8 Institutional logics strategizing.

capable to deal with them (Gümüsay et al., 2020a). This by itself can be professed as a profound strategic problem, giving a whole new meaning to the notion of competition. Rather than firms competing with each other on the basis of their competitive advantage, organizations find their environmental survival process is about accommodating competing institutional logics to remain viable (see Figure 8). It is also interesting that economics is considered as just another logic. Instead of separating out competitiveness and legitimacy as was done in IB/S (e.g. Peng, 2003), Non-Market Strategy (e.g. Baron, 1995a), and by Oliver (1997a) in New Institutionalism, being competitive is about being legitimate in terms of an institutional logic informed by the principles of economics.

Strategic choice is present by way of the assumption that actors because of the contradictions are to be able to pick and choose which institutional logic they want to adhere too. However, the extent of strategic choice is qualified at the micro level by way of people only working with institutional logics that come to mind, and at the meso level by way of the localized organizational practices that happen to be present. Overall, institutionalization is the consequence of distributed agency.

8 Understanding Institutionalization: Institutional Work and Constant Becoming

The notion of institutional entrepreneurship tries to deal with the lack of strategic agency that was inherent in New Institutionalism and particularly in the isomorphism thesis. It turned institutionalization into an episodic process of institutional change interspersed with periods of stability happening mostly at the level of the organizational field. A similar sequencing was presented as happening within firms and organizations with convergent incremental change alternating with radical strategic change. The notion of institutional logics prompted a recognition of institutional complexity: a situation where people and organizations are confronted with multiple and often conflicting institutionalized arrangements. Institutional work as another variant of institutional theory initially picked up on institutional entrepreneurship, to not only concentrate on change but also on continuity; on how institutional arrangements change but also stay in place as a consequence of deliberate and purposeful activity (Lawrence & Suddaby, 2006; Lawrence et al., 2009;; Lawrence et al., 2011). In short, institutional work is about institutionalization.

Scandinavian Institutionalism (Boxenbaum & Pedersen, 2009; Sahlin & Wedlin, 2008) as an alternative form of the institutional work approach resulted in a different and more performative understanding of institutionalization, with institutionalized arrangements seen as an accomplishment and the result of unceasing activity that generates an effect of continuity and change. Work by Smets and colleagues ended up in a similar position (Smets & Jarzabkowski, 2013; Smets et al., 2012; Smets et al., 2015b; Smets et al., 2017). What they labelled as practice-driven institutionalism sees institutions continuously being recreated as practices are being enacted, especially because they recognize the presence of multiple institutional logics. The performative variant of institutional work turns institutionalization into a continuous 'becoming' with institutions appearing 'as momentary effects of and for action' (Bjerregaard & Jonasson, 2014: 1510).

'Becoming' contrast with 'being' as referring to fundamentally different views on the nature of reality. 'Being' captures a substantialist ontology with reality understood as consisting of entities to which change happens. This is very much present in all other institutional theory variants. 'Becoming' offers an alternative ontology where everything is seen as coming into existence because of an underlying process. What we experience as entities is the consequence of a process generating something that appears to have some persistence over time.

On introducing the concept of 'institutional work' Lawrence and Suddaby (2006: 215) define it as the 'the purposive action of individuals and organizations aimed at creating, maintaining, and disrupting institutions'. Their answer to the paradox of embedded agency (Seo & Creed, 2002) is a variant of the leeway solution. They endow an individual person with reflexivity (Giddens, 1984) and therefore as being capable of dealing in a deliberate manner with the expectations that institutionalized arrangements in the field bring to a situation. This then allows for people being able to consider disrupting and recreating but also to decide to maintain an institution. By labelling it as 'work', they want to emphasize that institutionalization takes effort.

Lawrence and Suddaby (2006) distinguish between six activity types[3] by which an institution is maintained, and continuity generated. The 'enabling', 'policing', and 'deterring' activity types ensure that there is adherence to the institutionalized arrangements. The activity types of 'valorizing/demonizing', 'mythologizing', and 'embedding and routinizing' make that institutional arrangements are reproduced. Institutional change happens by way of disrupting existing arrangements and creating new ones. Creation requires political activity types like 'vesting', 'defining', and 'advocacy'. Such political activity reconstructs rules, property rights, and boundaries that regulate access to resources. There are reconstruction activity types like 'constructing identities', 'changing norms', and 'constructing networks' that recreate the belief system. Furthermore, there are boundary activity types that recreate abstract categorizations and regulate the boundaries of meaning systems. These activity types are 'mimicry', 'theorizing', and 'educating'. Institutional work aimed at disrupting an institution in effect attacks or undermines compliance. The activity types associated with disruption are 'disconnecting sanctions/rewards', 'disassociating moral foundations', and 'undermining assumptions and beliefs'.

The disruption and creation activity types are very reminiscent of how the process of institutional change was understood with institutional entrepreneurship. The maintenance activities that are responsible for institutional continuity is what the institutional work variant adds to institutional theory. It also turns institutionalization into more of an ongoing process with all the activity types being present, albeit not always to the same degree. As with institutional entrepreneurship, there have been many case studies, although mostly concentrating on the disruption and creation side of institutional work and less on the maintenance aspect (Lawrence et al., 2013). These include studies of the institutional work done for establishing management fashions and fads (Perkmann & Spicer, 2008), authority at San Francisco State College (Rojas, 2010), logging in British Columbia (Zietsma & Lawrence, 2010), cholesterol-lowering foods (Ritvala & Kleymann, 2012), the corporatization of law firms in the city of London (Empson et al., 2013), and the personal computer/Intel/Microsoft platform (Gawer & Phillips, 2013). Examples of institutional work maintenance cases are about specialist doctors remaining dominant in the English National Health Service (Currie et al., 2012), a responsible investment index (Slager et al., 2012), and crew selection for the Oxford-Cambridge boat race (Lok & de Rond, 2013).

---

[3] Lawrence and Suddaby utilize the term 'practices' here. To distinguish their approach to institutional work from the more performative practice-driven approach that will be introduced further down in this chapter, the term 'activity type' is used here.

Despite the variety of what is thought of as being institutionalized, as with institutional entrepreneurship the emphasis is on the patterned and regular activities rather than the norms, values, and ideas as being the crucial element of what constitutes an institution. How institutional work in terms of Lawrence and Suddaby (2006) is understood is also very similar to how institutional change and entrepreneurship have been elaborated, and to how strategic change has been presented to happen within organizations. The process is seen mostly as discursive. The contestation plays out by making claims and counterclaims of what is cognitively, normatively, and pragmatically legitimate by way of providing descriptions and voicing interpretations. The process principles predominantly are derived from structuration theory (Giddens, 1976, 1979, 1984) with institutionalization seen as structuration. However, in contrast to institutional entrepreneurship, the concept of institutional work covers both institutional change and institutional continuity. Moreover, the 'work' in institutional work signals that institutionalization is an ongoing process that continuously requires people to engage in maintenance, disruption, and re-creation activity. Furthermore, there is an acknowledgement that institutionalization and especially change initiatives are collective efforts rather than being attributable to a single institutional entrepreneur.

Mostly in parallel with Lawrence, Suddaby, and colleagues' efforts, Scandinavian Institutionalism developed and was recognized as an alternative form of institutional work (Boxenbaum & Pedersen, 2009; Sahlin & Wedlin, 2008). This alternative to institutional work developed from New Institutionalism in that it started with isomorphism as a core construct for understanding institutionalization, yet provided a twist as to how this transpires. Doing so, it arrived at a different and more performative understanding of how institutionalization happens. Initially, the process principles of social construction (Berger & Luckmann, 1966) underpinning New Institutionalism made way for sensemaking (Weick, 1979, 1995). Although both approaches have the same phenomenological roots, sensemaking concentrates on individual human actors as sensemakers and combines this with a requirement for people to have to make sense or understand what is going on for collective arrangements like organizations to function. Scandinavian Institutionalism took sensemaking into institutional theory to posit that people when confronted with institutional pressures have an ability to make sense of these pressures in different ways. Rather than expecting that institutionalized expectations turn almost inevitably into isomorphism as per DiMaggio and Powell (1983), the possibility of making sense differently would account for variability. There was even the suggestion of a form of strategic agency with people being aware of different possible interpretations to deliberately pick one that suits their interests. This is an argument that resonates with institutional logics.

With Czarniawska and Sevón (1996), Scandinavian Institutionalism orientated the process principles away from sensemaking. Instead, it started favouring actor-network theory and especially the notion of 'translation' (Callon, 1986; Callon & Latour, 1981; Latour, 1986). Translation is applied here as an alternative to diffusion (Boxenbaum & Pedersen, 2009; Brandtner, Powell, & Horvath, 2024; Sahlin & Wedlin, 2008; Zilber, 2006). The notion of diffusion assumes institutional pressures to be clear, unquestioned, and adhered to, and as such institutional requirements spread unaltered across the various organizations that are submitted to them. Translation sees adherence to institutional pressures as inherently problematic because these pressures are not necessarily clear and therefore require interpretation (as with sensemaking), but also adaptation, modification, and reshaping to accommodate and make them work within different organizations. Institutionalization as translation, therefore, is partly creative with the institutional expectations being re-imagined, to suit the situation, and is partly edited as elements of these expectations which are too problematic are discarded. This is regarded as institutional work because institutionalization as translation also requires effort. Moreover, there is intrinsic variability in how an institutionalized arrangement is made to bear upon an organization's activities.

Institutionalization as translation is performative (Callon, 1998; MacKenzie & Millo, 2003; Sevón, 1996). The basic premise is that an institution is not an independently existing set of norms, values, and ideas with associated appropriate patterns of activity to which people and organizations submit, and which people can reflect on to purposefully maintain, disrupt, and re-create as per Lawrence and Suddaby (2006). Instead, activities perform an institution. It is through activities that the effect of maintenance, adaptation, or disruption is generated. This means that institutionalized arrangements are always and continuously re-created as and when the patterned activities happen. In other words: institutions are always in a state of 'becoming' (Tsoukas & Chia, 2003). The norms, values, and ideas aspect of an institution can be described as the ostensive part by providing the idealized principles that describe the institution, while the patterned activities are the performative part as an institution's actual manifestation (Latour, 1986; Sevón, 1996).[4]

A similar development regarding institutional work is found with Smets and colleagues (Smets & Jarzabkowski, 2013; Smets et al., 2012; Smets et al., 2015b; Smets et al., 2017) who question the presupposition of purposefulness

---

[4] Feldman (2000) also utilizes this distinction in developing her notion of organizational routines in what later became known as 'routine dynamics'. The ostensive aspect of a routine provides an idealized description how it should be done; the performative aspect denotes how the routine is done.

in Lawrence and Suddaby's (2006) definition of institutional work. They argue that maintaining and changing institutionalized arrangements also can originate from people in organizations just going about doing their daily business of dealing with the day-to-day issues that they encounter. Adopting a practice-driven approach and drawing on Schatzki's (2001: 2) definition of a practice as 'embodied, materially mediated arrays of human activity centrally organized around shared practical understanding', practices are taken as norms and routines and differentiated from praxis as everyday performance, and from practitioners as the active embodiment of practices (Whittington, 2006). The difference between practices and praxis echoes the distinction between the ostensive and performative aspects of an institution.

Smets and colleagues also argue that institutional complexity or the simultaneous presence of conflicting institutional logics (Greenwood et al., 2011) is the normal state of affairs (see also Bjerregaard & Jonasson, 2014). Institutional logic is taken to refer to Schatzki's (2006) 'general understanding' or the overall justification why a practice is enacted there and then; an interpretation endorsed by Schatzki (2021). Logics are instantiated in praxis as practices are enacted (cf. Zilber, 2024). Institutional change then originates with the mundane practicality and associated improvisations of having to accommodate conflicting logics or practical understandings when practices are enacted. The improvisations indicate what each institutional logic means for enacting a practice there and then, which then can spread across other subsequent practice enactments in the organization's bundle.This is how Smets et al. (2012) and Smets and Jarzabkowski (2013) describe how lawyers marry the different demands of the legal profession in England and Germany when they established a bundle of blended practices that constitute a newly merged firm practicing international law. However, not every improvisation will result in institutional change of that magnitude. Sminia (2011) develops a very similar argument about collusion in the Dutch construction industry as a case of institutional continuity while its illegality poses a strong impetus for change. To Sminia (2011) and Smets et al. (2017) the main driver for performing practices, for dealing with institutional complexity, and therefore for institutional continuity and change is the practicality of 'getting the job done'. Emphasizing practicality as the main thrust for institutionalization moves the argument away from meaning (Lounsbury et al., 2021; Quatrone, 2015). Because this is a continuous effort, it fits the realm of institutional work.

Beunza and Ferraro (2019) pick up on the performativity of institutional work by observing that Scandinavian Institutionalism mostly concentrated on the discursive aspect of translation of making an institutional arrangement meaningful in a particular context. They argue there is a political aspect to performativity as well. For them, the politics of translation consists of the movements of 'problematization', 'interessement', 'enrolment', and 'mobilization' (Callon, 1986). Through problematization an institution takes shape as an ensemble of solutions that is presented as dealing with a range of problems and interests. This institution then presents an obligatory passage point for various actors as they become convinced of being stakeholders in this institution while they are pursuing their particular and often idiosyncratic interests. Interessement endows each stakeholder with an identity in terms of the institution. This identity tells them how they understand themselves and their interests in relation to this institution, what activities are expected from them, and how these activities contribute to meeting their interests. Enrolment happens when the stakeholders, having identified with their respective identities, act accordingly in pursuit of meeting the interests they have been associated with. Mobilization occurs when stakeholders identify and act in accordance with the institution to the extent that they become representable in terms of the institution. In this way, Beunza and Ferraro (2019) turn institutional work into performative work. Institutional performative work denotes an understanding of institutionalization as translation and as an unceasing effort of problematization, interessement, enrolment, and representation.

Beunza and Ferraro (2019) present institutional performative work as driven by a single actor or translator who carefully arranges for stakeholders to become problematized, interessemented, enrolled, and represented. In their empirical work, they concentrate on Charles (a pseudonym) who champions the development of a new product in a financial data company. Alternatively, Czarniawska (2009) presents institutional performative work as a collective endeavour with various actors – human and non-human – wittingly and unwittingly making contributions which happen to generate an institution. This is how she explains how the London School of Economics became established.

Both Scandinavian and Practice-driven Institutionalism suggest that institutions exist by way of the ongoing and never-ending institutional performative work or institutionalization that is taking place. Institutionalization then is about stabilization (Reinecke & Lawrence, 2023) with institutional performative work generating the patterned activity by which it exists – the performative aspect – accompanied by descriptions in terms of norms, values, and ideas – the ostensive or discursive aspect – by which it is legitimized. The focal point of institutional performative work and therefore of how to understand how an institution exists, then, are the practices that are enacted and turned into praxis by practitioners (cf. Lok & de Rond, 2013; Sminia, 2011). The suggestion also is to understand institutionalization as translation, as the problematization, interessement, enrolment, and mobilization by which an institution by way of practices takes shape performatively and discursively so that it provides identities and caters for the interests of the variety of actor/stakeholders who are then associated with and represented by this institution as practitioners.

From the perspective of institutional performative work, institutions are always in a state of becoming (cf. Tsoukas & Chia, 2003). Rather than processes like institutionalization, or continuity and change, happening to institutions as if these are independently existing entities, it is about institutionalization as a process with the patterning appreciable as continuity or change. Up to this point, every variant of institutional theory has adhered to what has been labelled as the 'weak' process approach, while institutional performative work is a variant of institutional theory that is more akin to the 'strong' process approach (Langley, 2009).

Furthermore and in contrast to Lawrence and Suddaby (2006), institutional performative work is not limited to the purposeful maintenance, adaptation, disruption, and recreation of an institution, although it can feature deliberate and intentional action of individual and collective actors to keep the process going. Institutional performative work offers a nuanced understanding of agency. Overall, the agency involved in institutionalization is proposed to be understood as an 'assemblage' (Latour, 2005): as an arrangement of human and non-human agency which in combination constitute the practices by which an institution comes into existence when these practices are enacted. To refer to this processual understanding of agency, the Deleuze and Guattari (1987) term of 'agencement' has been used (Beunza & Ferraro, 2019; Gehman et al., 2022; Raviola & Norbäck, 2013; Välikangas & Carlsen, 2020). According to Gherardi (2019a) the French word of 'agencement' appeared to be difficult to translate into English and maybe has been best described by her as 'establishing connections' between a mixture of human and non-human actors so that preformation can be generated. By using agencement it is recognized that institutionalization relies on distributed agency, requiring a coming together of many contributions from individual actors, collective agents, but also tangible and non-tangible material resources.

To account for human actors and how they can contribute deliberately, intentionally, and meaningfully to the agencement, Smets and Jarzabkowski (2013), Smets et al. (2017), and Raviola and Norbäck (2013) draw on Emirbayer and Mische (1998) and their distinction between iterative, projective, and practical-evaluative agency. Iterative agency with its orientation on the past appears when a practice is routinely enacted as it always has been and is therefore associated with performing institutional continuity. Projective agency with its orientation towards the future appears when a practice is enacted differently because a different performation is envisioned and is thus associated with institutional change. Practical-evaluative agency is orientated towards the present with issues dealt with in the here and now to account for the variability in praxis to accommodate different institutional logics and generates the plasticity or elasticity of any institutionalized arrangement (Bjerregaard & Jonasson, 2014; Boxenbaum & Pedersen, 2009; Lok & de Rond, 2013; Sahlin & Wedlin, 2008; Smets et al., 2015b).

Institutional work has been put forward to explain institutionalization. As defined and elaborated by Lawrence and Suddaby, institutionalization happens by way of various creating, maintaining, and disrupting activity types (Lawrence & Suddaby, 2006; Lawrence et al., 2009; Lawrence et al., 2011). The underpinning process principles that are referred to the most are structuration theory (Giddens, 1976, 1979, 1984). As such, the process is animated by reflexivity. The organizational strategy process essentially is doing the institutional work activities by which structuration is happening (see Figure 9). Lawrence and Suddaby (2006) purposely labelled it as 'work' to indicate that institutionalization requires continuous and – specific for them – deliberate effort. A strategist therefore is required to do this deliberate institutional work continuously. A departure from institutional entrepreneurship is that instead of the environmental process seeing institutionalization only happening by way of episodic change, institutional work envisions an ongoing process of institutionalization to maintain or change institutionalized arrangements.

Institutional performative work can happen unintentionally as well as deliberately. It borrows underpinning process principles from actor-network theory (Callon, 1998; Latour, 2005) and the theory of practice (Schatzki, 2002).

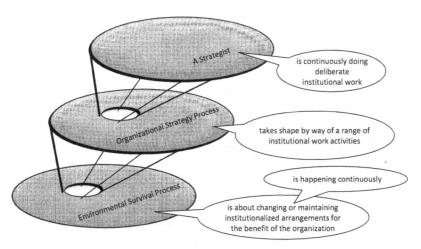

Figure 9 Institutional work strategizing.

Institutional performative work is another way of understanding how to accommodate institutional complexity (Greenwood et al., 2011) or the ever-presence of different and conflicting institutional logics. Accommodating differences happens as a matter of course when people go about doing what they do on a day-to-day basis. What they do is enacting practices and in doing so institutional logics are instantiated – adhered to, modified, dismissed – as the work is being done. The process is animated by teleoaffectivity (Schatzki, 2002) that tells a practitioner why a practice is to be enacted. Teleoaffectivity combines the practicality of 'getting the job done' (Smets et al., 2017) with affect or how much a practitioner cares about what needs to be done (Gherardi, 2019a). Adding affect resonates with the recent interest in the role of emotion in institutionalization (Friedland, 2018; Voronov & Vince, 2012).

Apart from translation and therefore institutionalization happening because of practices being enacted mundanely on a day-to-day basis, institutional performative work allows for the possibility of deliberately considered and attempted institutional change. On the one hand, Beunza and Ferraro (2019) present this as a single person – Charles, an executive at a financial data company – championing a new service that delivers data on environmental, social, and governance activity of companies to responsible investors – by him driving the translation to get this service up and running. This involves engaging with other executives in the company, people in his department, clients, responsible management activists but also with the data, to have all of this problematized, interessemented, enrolled, and mobilized.

On the other hand, Czarniawska (2009), writing about how the London School of Economics became established, presents institutionalization as translation as a collective effort, involving various instigators, supporters, users, opponents, money, a building, cups of tea, which all made contributions of some sort that translated a vague idea into a functioning university: an institution that is being performed by a range of different practices accompanied by specific norms, values, and ideas that legitimatize it. Among these ideas are accounts that effectively attribute leadership roles to specific human actors, despite some of them not having intended to play such a pivotal role.

These two contrasting accounts reveal a conceptual issue with institutional performative work. How can the iterative, projective, and practical-evaluative agency that individual human actors are endowed with as they are contributing to the enactment of a practice be squared with the agencement that is what allows a practice to be performed? More particularly, how is individual human agency to be singled out as possibly strategic agency while enacting a practice relies on all of this connected human and non-human agency? Beunza and Ferraro (2019) single out Charles as a strategist or strategy practitioner whose agency drives the process. Czarniawska (2009) provides a tale of agencement. In a way, we appear to have encountered the paradox of embedded agency again, albeit in a different form.

The conceptual solution that is on offer here is to treat the agency with which a human actor is endowed with and the agencement that is assembled in a practice as basically the same story, but only if there is full translation. In actor-network theory, full translation is referred to as being blackboxed (Latour, 2005). A practice is a black box when all human and non-human actors relevant for this practice are problematized, interessemented, enrolled, and mobilized so that the agencement is present. This happens when a practice performs because the whole of the agencement acts. Without being blackboxed, individual human actors will not have agency and a practice will not perform. A human actor like Charles in Beunza and Ferraro's (2019) case, in being singled out/singling himself out as a strategist, he is denoted/declares himself as representing strategy practices when strategy practices are being enacted. It is as if the strategy practices are being performed on his behalf. This can be any practice that is enacted while championing this new product in a financial data company and among those who are designated to become customers. Charles relies on translation to be a translator.

One of these practices, for instance, is formulating a business plan for the new product. Enacting such a practice brings together Charles who thinks up the text, the computer that processes all the words, the data that speaks in favour of the new product, the analytical frameworks by which the data are presented as a compelling argument, other people, procedures, equipment that produce this data, and more. This all comes together as an agencement, and allows for Charles to be understood – and to understand himself – as a strategist exercising iterative, projective, and practical-evaluative agency (see Figure 10).

If Czarniawska (2009) would be about the same case, she would not have singled out Charles as a strategist driving the process. She would have mentioned him along all the other human and non-human agents that are present in the agencement. In this way, neither account is mutually exclusive. With both accounts, the organizational strategy process can be characterized as strategy-in -practices (MacKay et al., 2021) that combines the practical coping of practices being performed on a day-to-day basis with a the deliberate politics of practicality of discursively making claims and counterclaims about what is cognitively, normatively, and pragmatically legitimate and – maybe more importantly – performative experimentation that aims to demonstrate legitimacy by enacting (modified) practices.

Understanding the strategy process as institutional performative work, with a strategist seen as a practitioner exercising iterative, projective, and practical-evaluative agency, the organizational strategy process takes shape as strategy-in

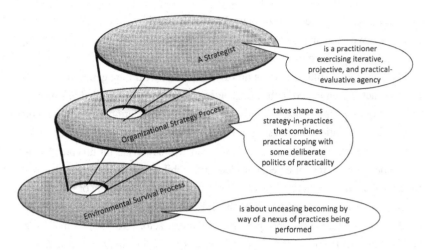

Figure 10 Institutional performative work strategizing.

-practices that combines practical coping with some deliberate politics of practicality. The environmental survival process then can be understood as the constant becoming of a nexus of practices (Schatzki, 2002) that are being enacted. The viability of a firm or an organization is then a matter of being denotable as representing some of these practices, as these are blackboxed through translation (Latour, 2005).

9 Discussion and Conclusion: Three Strategic Management Styles

It is possible to tell the story of institutional theory as an ongoing progression of insight as was done by Glynn and D'Aunno (2023), presenting this development as providing an increasingly improving understanding of what institutions do and of how institutionalization happens in the realm of management and organization. Such an argumentation would present the sociology-based variants of Old Institutionalism, New Institutionalism, institutional entrepreneurship and change, intra-organizational institutionalization, institutional logics, and institutional work as subsequent attempts at providing an ever-more sophisticated account, with each variant picking up problems and addressing issues inherent in earlier variants. We could even fit the economics-based variant of NIE in it somewhere as making a contribution. Alternatively, we could present the proliferation of so many different variants as evidence of the conceptual mess that institutional theory has developed into (Alvesson & Spicer, 2019).

A story of increasing insight would turn institutional theory into a unified approach. Utilizing what institutional theory teaches us it would allow us to propose a more synoptic approach to strategic management. To do that we would have to fudge the exact chronology of publication dates and glance over the more fundamental differences between the different variants. These differences include whether an institution is a cognitive or a social phenomenon, whether an institution essentially is about norms, values, and ideas or about patterned recurrent and regular activity, and if it is about norms, values, and ideas whether an institution only refers to formal rules and regulations or does it also include informal expectations. There is also a question whether an institution is a multilevel phenomenon, and if so, how many levels do we need to distinguish and how do these levels interact? Or is institutionalization a process that happens in the same way across individuals, organizations, fields, and societies, eliminating the need to distinguish between levels? Besides, we have come across six different solutions to the paradox of embedded agency: leeway, imperfect institutionalization, separation of agency and structure over time, exogenous shock, hybridity, and blackboxing. Institutionalization has been presented as episodic change upsetting periods of institutional continuity and as a rather fragile stabilization of what essentially is a process of continuous becoming, happening either because of the activities of an individual institutional entrepreneur or as a collective effort. Moreover, underlying process principles vary from methodological individualism, social construction, and structuration theory to actor-network theory and the theory of practice, and more.

When we concentrate on how all of this has been brought to bear upon strategic management, it is possible to delineate between three different strategic management styles. Rather than distinguishing between theoretical approaches by specifying constructs and relationships, style denotes a more aesthetic sensitivity by providing a distinctive account that you recognize when you see it (Gherardi, 2019b). In a way, institutional theory provides us with a choice of how you would like your strategic management to be. The three styles of understanding and doing strategic management are derived from some of the fundamental differences that are present between the many variants of institutional theory. These three styles can be labelled as competitiveness-based, legitimacy-based, and performativity-based. Each of these three strategic management styles can be a reference point for a strategist's 'theory-in-use' (Argyris & Schön, 1978); of how they prefer to understand themselves, the strategy process, and the environment, that is, their own strategic management style. These styles are also indicative of different ways in which strategic management research could develop.

Competitiveness-based strategic management sticks with Porter's (1980: 1) assumption that 'Competition is at the core of the success or failure of firms'.

Institutional theory here enhances textbook strategizing of dealing with competition by way of formulating and executing a strategy, with strategists engaged in processing relevant information to make rational decisions. Apart from information about the competitive environment and the firm's capabilities, there is also information about the institutional environment that needs consideration, albeit all in aid of a firm's competitiveness. This form of strategic management is evident in Non-Market Strategy and in the application of institutional theory in IB/S. NIE fits here as well, pointing at the importance of minimizing transaction costs. There is a bias here towards for-profit firms, although it can be claimed that non-profit and government organizations also face competition in some shape or form.

The bulk of mainstream strategic management research would fall within this realm because it is primarily concerned with competitive advantage. Institutional theory can and has provided further variables by which to explain competitive advantage and performance (e.g. Bonardi et al., 2006; Pajunen, 2008; Peng et al., 2008). This research mostly relied on NIE and to a lesser extent on New Institutionalism. It also limited the meaning of institution to formalized rules as put forward by governments and other (semi-)legislative bodies. If differences between institutional demands are acknowledged as per institutional logics, it is between countries. Institutional theory could tell mainstream strategy research that there is more to institutions than formal rules on a country-by-country basis. The set of institutional theory deduced variables to explain performance differences can be expanded to also include more informal norms, values, and ideas, and these sets of variables can be hypothesized and tested to vary between different settings than just countries (cf. Doh et al., 2012). Taking this up, corporate political activity – ironically – already has been recognized as possibly normatively illegitimate on the basis of a New Institutionalism argument because it goes against a norm of private interests not interfering with public concerns (Lim, 2023). Using institutional theory as a source for more variables for explaining competitive advantage adds to and submits to mainstream strategy research, propagating a strategic management that is primarily understood as a process of formulating and executing a strategic plan.

Legitimacy-based strategic management treats the way in which firms can be competitive as resulting from the regularity in activity and the accompanying norms, values, and ideas as these have been institutionalized. Rather than limiting strategy to the question how to compete, it should primarily concern itself with the institutionalized arrangements within which competition unfolds. There are two concurrent concerns that a strategist then should pay attention to. One concern is that institutional entrepreneurship and change as well as intra-organizational institutionalization tells us that any institutionalized arrangement is always liable to be changed, undermining the competitiveness a firm might have or possibly making it obsolete. This also points at the possibility of a firm choosing to become institutionally entrepreneurial to change the institutionalized arrangements in their favour. The other concern is that institutional logics tell us that there are several different and conflicting institutionalized arrangements putting demands upon every organization. Despite accommodating different logics with the various tactics that have been identified, there is a continuous risk of a firm failing on specific institutionalized expectations and consequently loosing legitimacy to the extent that its existence is being threatened.

Non-profit and public organizations would not necessarily be worried that much about their competitiveness, yet their legitimacy is similarly fragile because, in Old Institutionalism terms, their viability depends on how well they meet changing and multiple expectations of the several communities that they are serving.

Institutional change and entrepreneurship and intra-organizational change also tell us to expect that periods of change are alternated with periods of relative stability or continuity. Institutional logics tell us that organizations have some leeway in picking which institutionalized expectations to concentrate on. Organizations are also to some extent able to appear to be conforming to different expectations. This suggests there are pockets of institutional stability and continuity in space and time within which an organization can legitimately function for as long as these pockets exist. Such pockets will see the isomorphism of New Institutionalism appearing with organizations displaying convergent incremental change. It is within such pockets that for firms, much of the theorizing about competitive advantage from mainstream strategic management can still be useful. It also suggests there always is an existential threat of these pockets disappearing or changing to such an extent that more radical strategic change is required.

Overall, the continuity and change that emerges will be the result of the institutional work that everybody will be engaging in, with organizations required to take an active interest in conducting such work as part of their strategic management. This is where the legitimacy-based style comes into its own as actively acknowledging, dealing with and possibly initiating change, with competitiveness-based strategic management only applying if there is a prolonged period of institutional continuity. Rather than seeing strategy theory as centred on explaining competitive advantage, the theorizing would focus on understanding how organizations remain legitimate under conflicting and ever-changing institutional demands.

This sketch of legitimacy-based strategic management glosses over some of the conceptual discrepancies between the variants of institutional theory that are being drawn on. Putting these aside, what we have is an opportunity to develop institutional theory into a strategy theory to create a more sociologically informed research program to balance out the strategy scholarship that is based on economics, which still dominates the field. This would be a deviation from mainstream strategy research, with institutional theory offering a promising alternative to understanding how organizations realize strategy, with it being conceptualized as a process of managing emerging change rather than a process of deliberate choice (Mintzberg et al., 1990). One research avenue, for instance, could develop a concept like dynamic capability as a capability for institutionalization, institutional entrepreneurship, and institutional change. Core capabilities are already recognized as being a 'routine' (Grant, 1991; Nelson & Winter, 1982). The obvious step is to conceptualize a core capability as an institutionalized activity pattern and to investigate the development, maintenance, and change of core capabilities, that is, dynamic capability as requiring institutional work. This could also be beneficial for institutional theory itself by shedding light on the efficacy of institutional work. Lawrence and Suddaby (2006) have pointed out the presence and presumed effects of institutional work, yet we know little about what it is about creation, maintenance, and disruption work that generates the creation, maintenance, and disruption effects.

Research in strategic change and under the header of Strategy-as-Practice, which has chimed with institutional theory, already mostly fits with the legitimacy-based style of strategic management. However, it has mostly concentrated on the organizational strategy process and the activities of individual strategists. There are possibilities to make connections with the environmental survival process, basically by investigating strategy realization as a process that sees competing and surviving in the environment, organizational strategizing, and strategists' behaviour as an institutionalization process. This would be especially useful for Strategy-as-Practice for this would allow it to start theorizing more about how what strategists and organizations do links up with organizational performance, albeit in terms of legitimacy and the pockets of relative stability within which competitiveness plays out. There has been criticism that Strategy-as-Practice has lost sight of this essential element of strategy (Johnson et al., 2003; Sminia & de Rond, 2012).

Performativity-based strategic management as a style for understanding and enacting the process and as a research stream is still in its infancy (Cabantous et al., 2018; Guérard et al., 2013). It moves away from the substantialist approach to management and scholarship of 'weak' process, which characterizes the other two styles. Instead, entities like institutions are taken as essentially processual as these exist because of the activity by which these come into being. This means that strategy like performativity is an ongoing journey (Garud et al., 2018): a journey of ongoing institutionalization.

Although there are hints of performativity in the Institutional Logics perspective, this would mostly draw on ideas present in institutional performative work. This variant of institutional theory offers an even more radical departure from mainstream strategy. Strategic management then is more of a wayfinding that happens as you go along with the focus on keeping the organization underway while the institutionalization is happening rather than reaching pre-formulated destinations (Chia & Holt, 2023). A performative style of strategic management would be characterized as a continuous questioning and problem-solving (Sminia, 2022), but also as inherently generative and creative because institutions are constantly being recreated. This provides a striking contrast with the planning mode that effectively tells you to think up problems and solve them in advance, as if you know what will be happening. Wayfinding acknowledges that the future still has to happen and that it is strategy's job to help an organization travel into it. Wayfinding recognizes that a future is actively created with organizations making contributions as emerging issues are being dealt with.

Research that fits the performative style of strategic management is being conducted under the Strategy-as-Practice label. This concentrates mostly on organizational strategy process and sees it happening by way of enacting specific strategy practices. Such strategy practices include the many tools and techniques that are present in the strategy textbooks. However, from a performativity angle these are not analytical and cognitive aids to formulate a plan to be subsequently executed. What is put forward is that strategy tools and techniques provide a language of strategy by which the discursive aspect of the politics of practicality plays out (Kornberger & Clegg, 2011; Ligonie, 2018). Furthermore, something like a strategic plan can become a non-human actor and part of the agencement of strategy-in-practices (MacKay et al., 2021). In this way, strategy formulation already is strategy implementation by bringing strategy into action (Sminia & Valdovinos, 2022). Additional research would look into the day-to-day coping of the strategy-in-practices (MacKay et al., 2021), which is going on beyond the deliberate strategy practices that are being enacted. Chia and Mackay (2023) have already proposed for this mundane day-to-day practical coping to be understood as dynamic capability. An intriguing question then is how the deliberate practicing of strategy practices resonates with the practical coping of strategy-in-practices?

Another question that warrants further research zooms out to the organizational survival process. Here the performative aspect of institutional performative work comes into play with the way in which an organization performs its bundle of practices (Schatzki, 2005). This is a matter of what practices are present in the bundle, their agencement as a connection of human and non-human agency, but also how these are being enacted, given the iterative, projective, and practical-evaluative agency that is available. Because practice theory tends to be based on a flat ontology by seeing everything as one process rather than distinguishing between multiple levels of different but connected processes (Seidl & Whittington, 2014), this is not about how the organization interacts with the environment. Enacting the bundle of practices by which the organization exists happens within many other practices in the nexus of practices being enacted, all as part of the same basic process.

Suggestions are that strategy practices make their contribution only if these inspire other practices in the bundle by which an organization exists to be enacted differently and when these experimentations appear to make a difference (Merkus et al., 2019; Sminia & Valdovinos, 2022; Vargha, 2018). However, the difference which is then generated has to resonate beyond the bundle of practices by which the organization exists, to also be of some practicality in the wider nexus of practices of the organizational survival process. How that is happening and can be made to happen is still largely unexplored. Overall, research inspired by this performative-style would focus on how organizations practically contribute to an ever-changing world.

Having consulted institutional theory, we have ended up with three different strategic management styles: competitiveness-bases, legitimacy-based, and performativity-based. For each style, institutional theory has something to contribute, albeit by drawing on specific variants. Overall, the potential that institutional theory shows for the further development of the strategic management field, for both theory and practice, is that there is much more to strategy than what the basic textbook approach continuous to tell us. There is much more to strategy than dealing with competition.

References

Abell, P., Felin, T., & Foss, N. 2008. Building micro-foundations for the routines, capabilities, and performance links. *Managerial and Decision Economics*, 29: 489–501.

Alvesson, M., Hallett, T., & Spicer, A. 2019. Uninhibited institutionalisms. *Journal of Management Inquiry*, 28(2): 119–127.

Alvesson, M., & Spicer, A. 2019. Neo-institutional theory and organization studies: A mid-life crisis? *Organization Studies*, 40(2): 199–218.

Ansoff, H. I. 1965. *Corporate Strategy*. New York: McGraw Hill.

Argyris, C., & Schön, D. A. 1978. *Organizational Learning: A Theory of Action Perspective*. Reading, MA: Addison-Wesley.

Balogun, J., & Johnson, G. 2005. From intended strategies to unintended outcomes: The impact of change recipient sensemaking. *Organization Studies*, 26(11): 1573–1601.

Barley, S. R., & Tolbert, P. S. 1997. Institutionalization and structuration: Studying the links between action and institution. *Organization Studies*, 18(1): 93–117.

Barney, J. B. 1986. Strategic factor markets: Expectations, luck, and business strategy. *Management Science*, 32(10): 1231–1241.

Baron, D. P. 1995a. Integrated strategy: Market and nonmarket components. *California Management Review*, 37(2): 47–65.

Baron, D. P. 1995b. The nonmarket strategy system. *Sloan Management Review* (Fall): 73–85.

Bass, B. M. 1991. From transactional to transformational leadership: Learning to share the vision. *Organizational Dynamics*, 18(3): 19–31.

Battilana, J., & Casciaro, T. 2012. Change agents, networks, and institutions: A contingency theory of organizational change. *Academy of Management Journal*, 55(2): 819–836.

Battilana, J., & Dorado, S. 2010. Building sustainable hybrid organizations: The case of commercial microfinance organizations. *Academy of Management Journal*, 53: 1419–1440.

Battilana, J., Leca, B., & Boxenbaum, E. 2009. How actors change institutions: Towards a theory of institutional entrepreneurship. *Academy of Management Annals*, 3(1): 65–107.

Beckert, J. 1999. Agency, entrepreneurs, and institutional change: The role of strategic choice and institutionalized practices in organizations. *Organization Studies*, 20(5): 777–799.

Bennis, W., & Nanus, B. 1985. *Leaders: The Strategies for Taking Charge.* New York: Harper & Row.

Berger, P. L., & Luckmann, T. 1966. *The Social Construction of Reality: A Treatise in the Sociology of Knowledge.* New York: Anchor Books.

Beunza, D., & Ferraro, F. 2019. Performative work: Bridging performativity and institutional theory in the responsible investment field. *Organization Studies*, 40(4): 515–543.

Bhappu, A. D. 2000. The Japanese family: An institutional logic for Japanese corporate networks and Japanese management. *Academy of Management Review*, 25(2): 409–515.

Binder, A. 2007. For love and money: Organizations' creative responses to multiple environmental logics. *Theory and Society*, 36: 547–571.

Bjerregaard, T., & Jonasson, C. 2014. Managing unstable institutional contradictions: The work of becoming. *Organization Studies*, 35(10): 1507–1536.

Blau, P. M. 1974. *On the Nature of Organizations.* New York: Wiley.

Boddewyn, J., & Doh, J. P. 2011. Global strategy and the collaboration of MNEs, NGOs, and governments for the provision of collective goods in emerging markets. *Global Strategy Journal*, 1: 345–361.

Bonardi, J.-P., Hillman, A. J., & Keim, G. D. 2005. The attractiveness of political markets: Implications for firm strategy. *Academy of Management Review*, 30(3): 397–413.

Bonardi, J.-P., Holburn, G. L. F., & Vanden Bergh, R. G. 2006. Nonmarket strategy performance: Evidence from US electric utilities. *Academy of Management Journal*, 49(6): 1209–1228.

Bourdieu, P. 1977. *Outline of a Theory of Practice.* Cambridge: Cambridge University Press.

Bourdieu, P. 1990. *The Logic of Practice.* Cambridge: Polity Press.

Boxenbaum, E., & Pedersen, J. S. 2009. Scandinavian institutionalism: A case of institutional work. In T. B. Lawrence, R. Suddaby, & B. Leca (Eds.), *Institutional Work: Actors and Agency in Institutional Studies of Organization*: 178–204. Cambridge: Cambridge University Press.

Boyd, R., & Richardson, P. J. 1985. *Culture and the Evolutionary Process.* Chicago: University of Chicago Press.

Brandtner, C., Powell, W. W., & Horvath, A. 2024. From iron cage to glass house: Repurposing of bureaucratic management and the turn to openness. *Organization Studies*, 25(2), 193–221.

Brunsson, N. 2007. *The Consequences of Decision-Making.* Oxford: Oxford University Press.

Cabantous, L., Gond, J.-P., & Wright, A. 2018. The performativity of strategy: Taking stock and moving ahead. *Long Range Planning*, 51: 407–416.

Callon, M. 1986. Some elements of a sociology of translation: Domestication of the scallops and the fishermen of St. Brieuc Bay. In J. Law (Ed.), *Power, Action and Belief*: 196–233. London: Routledge.

Callon, M. 1998. *The Laws of the Markets*. Oxford: Basil Blackwell.

Callon, M., & Latour, B. 1981. Unscrewing the big leviathan: How actors macro-structure reality and how sociologists help them to do so. In K. Knorr-Cetina, & A. V. Cicourel (Eds.), *Advances in Social Theory and Methodology*: 277–303. Boston, MA: Routledge.

Campbell, A. 1987. Mission statements. *Long Range Planning*, 30(6): 931–932.

Chia, R., & Holt, R. 2023. Strategy, intentionality and success: Four logics for explaining strategic action. *Organization Theory*, 4(1): 1–25.

Chia, R. C. H., & Mackay, D. 2023. *Strategy-in-Practices*. Cambridge: Cambridge University Press.

Child, J. 1972. Organisational structure, environment and performance: The role of strategic choice. *Sociology*, 6(1): 1–22.

Child, J., & Smith, C. 1987. The context and process of organizational transformation – Cadbury limited in its sector. *Journal of Management Studies*, 24(6): 565–593.

Coleman, J. 1990. *Foundations of Social Theory*. Cambridge, MA: Harvard University Press.

Commons, J. R. 1934. *Institutional Economics*. Maddison: University of Madison Press.

Coule, T., & Patmore, B. 2013. Institutional logics, institutional work, and public service innovation in non-profit organizations. *Public Administration*, 91(4): 980–997.

Currie, G., Lockett, A., Finn, R., Martin, G., & Waring, J. 2012. Institutional work to maintain professional power: Recreating the model of medical professionalism. *Organization Studies*, 33(7): 937–962.

Cyert, R. L., & March, J. G. 1963. *A Behavioral Theory of the Firm*. Englewood Cliffs, NJ: Prentice Hall.

Czarniawska, B. 2009. Emerging institutions: Pyramids or anthills. *Organization Studies*, 30(4): 423–441.

Czarniawska, B., & Sevón, G. (Eds.). 1996. *Translating Organizational Change*. Berlin: Walter de Gruyter.

de Figueirdo, J. M. 2009. Integrated political strategy. In J. A. Nickerson, & B. Silverman (Eds.), *Advances in Strategic Management – Economic Institutions in Strategy*, Vol. 26: 459–486. Bingley: Emerald.

Deleuze, G., & Guattari, F. 1987. *A Thousand Plateaus* (B. Massumi, Trans.). Minneapolis, MN: University of Minnesota Press.

Delmas, M. A., & Toffel, M. W. 2008. Organizational responses to environmental demands: Opening the black box. *Strategic Management Journal*, 29: 1027–1055.

DiMaggio, P. J. 1988. Interest and agency in institutional theory. In L. Zucker (Ed.), *Institutional Patterns and Organizations*: 3–32. Cambridge, MA: Ballinger.

DiMaggio, P. J., & Powell, W. W. 1983. The iron cage revisited: Institutional isomorphism and collective rationality in organizational fields. *American Sociological Review*, 48(2): 147–160.

DiMaggio, P. J., & Powell, W. W. 1991. Introduction. In W. W. Powell, & P. J. DiMaggio (Eds.), *The New Institutionalism in Organizational Analysis*: 1–38. Chicago: Chicago University Press.

Doh, J. P., Lawton, T. C., & Rajwani, T. 2012. Advancing nonmarket strategy research: Institutional perspectives in a changing world. *Academy of Management Perspectives*, 26(3) (August): 22–39.

Domínguez, B., Gómez, J., & Maícas, J. P. in press. When does high institutional quality explain the presence of multinational enterprises in a foreign country? Experiential and vicarious learning as boundary conditions. *Strategic Organization*. https://doi.org/10.1177/14761270231195497.

Dorado, S. 2005. Institutional entrepreneurship, partaking, and convening. *Organization Studies*, 26(3): 385–414.

Dorobantu, S., Kaul, A., & Zelner, B. 2017. Nonmarket strategy research through the lens of new institutional economics: An integrative review and future directions. *Strategic Management Journal*, 38: 114–140.

Emirbayer, M., & Mische, A. 1998. What is agency? *American Journal of Sociology*, 103(4): 962–1023.

Empson, L., Cleaver, I., & Allen, J. 2013. Managing partners and management professionals: Institutional work dyads in professional partnerships. *Journal of Management Studies*, 50(5): 808–844.

Feldman, M. S. 2000. Organizational routines as a source of continuous change. *Organization Science*, 11(6): 611–629.

Feldman, M. S. 2003. A performative perspective on stability and change in organizational routines. *Industrial and Corporate Change*, 12(4): 727–752.

Feldman, M. S., & Pentland, B. T. 2003. Reconceptualizing organizational routines as a source of flexibility and change. *Administrative Science Quarterly*, 48(1): 94–118.

Felin, T., & Foss, N. 2009. Organizational routines and capabilities: Historical drift and a course-correction toward microfoundations. *Scandinavian Journal of Management*, 25: 157–167.

Fligstein, N. 1997. Social skill and institutional theory. *American Behavioral Scientist*, 40(4): 397–405.

Fligstein, N. 2001. Social skill and the theory of fields. *Sociological Theory*, 19(2): 105–125.

Foss, N. J. (Ed.). 1997. *Resources, Firms, and Strategies: A Reader in the Resource-based Perspective*. Oxford: Oxford University Press.

Friedland, R. 2018. Moving institutional logics forward: Emotion and meaningful material practice. *Organization Studies*, 39(4): 515–542.

Friedland, R., & Alford, R. R. 1991. Bringing society back in: Symbols, practices, and institutional contradictions. In W. W. Powell, & P. J. DiMaggio (Eds.), *The New Institutionalism in Organizational Analysis*: 232–263. Chicago: University of Chicago Press.

Garcia-Pont, C., & Nohria, N. 2002. Local versus global mimetism: The dynamics of alliance formation in the automobile industry. *Strategic Management Journal*, 23: 307–321.

Garud, R., Gehman, J., & Tharchen, T. 2018. Performativity as ongoing journeys: Implications for strategy, entrepreneurship, and innovation. *Long Range Planning*, 51): 500–509.

Garud, R., Jain, S., & Kumaraswamy, A. 2002. Institutional entrepreneurship in the sponsorship of common technological standards: The case of Sun Microsystems and Java. *Academy of Management Journal*, 45(1): 196–214.

Gawer, A., & Phillips, N. 2013. Institutional work as logics shift: The case of Intel's transformation to platform leader. *Organization Studies*, 34(8): 1035–1071.

Gehman, J., Sharma, G., & Beveridge, A. 2022. Theorizing institutional entrepereneuring: Arborescent and rhizomatic assembling. *Organization Studies*, 43(2): 289–310.

Getz, K. A. 1997. Research in corporate political action: Integration and assessment. *Business & Society*, 36(1): 32–72.

Gherardi, S. 2019a. *How to Conduct a Practice-based Study: Problems and Methods* (2nd ed.). Cheltenham: Edward Elgar.

Gherardi, S. 2019b. Theorizing affective ethnography for organization studies. *Organization*, 26(6): 741–760.

Giddens, A. 1976. *New Rules of Sociological Method: A Positive Critique of Interpretative Sociologies*. London: Hutchinson.

Giddens, A. 1979. *Central Problems in Social Theory: Action, Structure and Contradiction in Social Analysis*. Basingstoke: Macmillan.

Giddens, A. 1984. *The Constitution of Society: Outline of a Theory of Structuration*. Cambridge: Polity Press.

Glynn, M. A., & D'Aunno, T. 2023. An intellectual history of institutional theory: Looking back to move forward. *Academy of Management Annals*, 17(1): 1–30.

Goodrick, E., & Salancik, G. R. 1996. Organizational discretion in responding to institutional practices: Hospitals and cesarean births. *Administrative Science Quarterly*, 41: 1–28.

Granovetter, M. 1985. Economic action and social structure. *American Journal of Sociology*, 91(3): 481–510.

Grant, R. M. 1991. The Resource-based theory of competitive advantage: Implications for strategy formulation. *California Management Review*, 33(3): 114–135.

Greenwood, R., & Hinings, C. R. 1988. Organizational design types, tracks and the dynamics of strategic change. *Organization Studies*, 9(3): 293–316.

Greenwood, R., & Hinings, C. R. 1993. Understanding strategic change: The contribution of archetypes. *Academy of Management Journal*, 36(5): 1052–1081.

Greenwood, R., & Hinings, C. R. 1996. Understanding radical organizational change: Bringing together the old and the new institutionalism. *Academy of Management Review*, 21(4): 1022–1054.

Greenwood, R., Oliver, C., Sahlin, K., & Suddaby, R. (Eds.). 2008. *The SAGE Handbook of Organizational Institutionalism*. Los Angeles, CA: Sage.

Greenwood, R., Raynor, M. E., Kodelj, H., Micelotta, E. R., & Lounsbury, M. 2011. Institutional complexity and organizational responses. *Academy of Management Annals*, 5(1): 1–55.

Greenwood, R., & Suddaby, R. 2006. Institutional entrepreneurship in mature fields: The big five accounting firms. *Academy of Management Journal*, 49(1): 27–48.

Greenwood, R., Suddaby, R., & Hinings, C. R. 2002. Theorizing change: The role of professional associations in the transformation of institutional fields. *Academy of Management Journal*, 45(1): 58–80.

Grinyer, P. H., Mayes, D., & McKiernan, P. 1988. *Sharpbenders: The Secrets of Unleashing Corporate Potential*. Oxford: Basil Blackwell.

Guérard, S., Langley, A., & Seidl, D. 2013. Rethinking the concept of performance in strategy research: Towards a performative perspective. *M@n@gement*, 16(5): 566–578.

Guler, I., Guillén, M. F., & Macpherson, J. M. 2002. Global competition, institutions, and the diffusion of organizational practices: The international spread of ISO 9000 quality certificates. *Administrative Science Quarterly*, 47: 207–232.

Gumpert, P. J. 2000. Academic restructuring: Organizational change and institutional imperatives, higher education. *International Journal of Higher Education and Educational Planning*, 39: 67–91.

Gümüsay, A. A., Claus, L., & Amis, J. 2020a. Engaging with grand challenges: An institutional logics perspective. *Organization Theory*, 1: 1–20.

Gümüsay, A. A., Smets, M., & Morris, T. 2020b. 'God at work': Engaging central and incompatible institutional logics through elastic hybridity. *Academy of Management Journal*, 63(1): 124–154.

Hardy, C., & Maguire, S. 2008. Institutional entrepreneurship. In R. Greenwood, C. Oliver, K. Sahlin, & R. Suddaby (Eds.), *The SAGE Handbook of Organizational Institutionalism*: 198–217. London: Sage.

Hargadon, A. B., & Douglas, Y. 2001. When innovations meet institutions: Edison and the design of the electric light. *Administrative Science Quarterly*, 46: 476–501.

Haveman, H. A., & Rao, H. 1997. Structuring a theory of moral sentiments: Institutional and organizational coevolution in the early thrift industry. *American Journal of Sociology*, 102(6): 1606–1651.

Henisz, W. J., & Delios, A. 2004. Information or influence? The benefits of experience for managing political uncertainty. *Strategic Organization*, 2(4): 389–421.

Henisz, W. J., & Zelner, B. A. 2003. The strategic organization of political risks and opportunities. *Strategic Organization*, 1(4): 451–460.

Henisz, W. J., & Zelner, B. A. 2012. Strategy and competition in the market and nonmarket arenas. *Academy of Management Perspectives*, 26(3): 40–51.

Hillman, A. J., & Hitt, M. A. 1999. Corporate political strategy formulation: A model of approach, participation, and strategy decisions. *Academy of Management Review*, 24(4): 825–824.

Hinings, C. R., & Greenwood, R. 1988a. *The Dynamics of Strategic Change*. Oxford: Basil Blackwell.

Hinings, C. R., & Greenwood, R. 1988b. The normative prescription of organizations. In L. G. Zucker (Ed.), *Institutional Patterns and Organizations: Culture and Environment*: 53–70. Chicago, IL: Ballinger.

Hoffman, A. J. 1999. Institutional evolution and change: Environmentalism and the US chemical industry. *Academy of Management Journal*, 42(4): 351–371.

Hoffman, A. J. 2001. Linking organizational and field-level analysis. *Organization & Environment*, 14(2): 133–156.

Holburn, G. L. F., & Vanden Bergh, R. G. 2008. Making friends in hostile environments: Political strategy in regulated industries. *Academy of Management Review*, 23(2): 521–540.

Holm, P. 1995. The dynamics of institutionalization: Transformation processes in Norwegian fisheries. *Administrative Science Quarterly*, 40: 423–443.

Hotho, J. J., & Pedersen, T. 2012. Beyond the 'rules of the game': Three institutional approaches and how they matter for international business. In

G. Wood, & M. Demirbag (Eds.), *Handbook of Institutional Approaches to International Business*: 236–273. Cheltenham: Edward Elgar.

Hrebiniak, L. G., & Joyce, W. 1984. *Implementing Strategy*. New York: Macmillan.

Huff, A. S. 1982. Industry influences on strategy reformulation. *Strategic Management Journal*, 3: 119–131.

Ingram, P., & Silverman, B. (Eds.). 2002. *The New Institutionalism in Strategic Management*. Amsterdam: Elsevier.

Jarzabkowski, P. A., Balogun, J., & Seidl, D. 2007. Strategizing: The challenges of a practice perspective. *Human Relations*, 60(1): 5–27.

Jepperson, R. L. 1991. Institutions, institutional effects, and institutionalism. In W. W. Powell, & P. J. DiMaggio (Eds.), *The New Institutionalism in Organizational Analysis*: 143–163. Chicago: Chicago University Press.

Johnson, G. 1987. *Strategic Change and the Management Process*. Oxford: Basil Blackwell.

Johnson, G., Melin, L., & Whittington, R. 2003. Micro strategy and strategizing: Towards an activity-based view. *Journal of Management Studies*, 40(1): 3–22.

Jones, C., & Livne-Tarandach, R. 2008. Designing a frame: Rhetorical strategies of architects. *Journal of Organizational Behavior*, 29: 1075–1099.

Kaplan, R. S., & Norton, D. P. 1996. *The Balanced Scorecard: Translating Strategy into Action*. Boston, MA: Harvard Business School Press.

Khaire, M., & Wadhwani, R. D. 2010. Changing landscapes: The construction of meaning and value in a new market category – modern Indian art. *Academy of Management Journal*, 53(6): 1281–1304.

Kikulis, L. M., Slack, T., & Hinings, C. R. 1992. Institutionally specific design archetypes: A framework for understanding change in National Sport Organizations. *International Review for the Sociology of Sport*, 27: 343–369.

Kikulis, L. M., Slack, T., & Hinings, C. R. 1995. Sector-specific patterns of organizational design change. *Journal of Management Studies*, 32(1): 67–100.

Kingsley, A. F., Vanden Bergh, R. G., & Bonardi, J.-P. 2012. Political markets and regulatory uncertainty: Insights and implications for integrated strategy. *Academy of Management Perspectives*, 26(3) (August): 52–67.

Kondra, A. Z., & Hinings, C. R. 1998. Organizational diversity and change in institutional theory. *Organization Studies*, 19(5): 743–767.

Kondra, A. Z., & Hurst, D. C. 2009. Institutional processes of organizational culture. *Culture and Organization*, 15(1): 39–58.

Kornberger, M., & Clegg, S. R. 2011. Strategy as performative practice. *Strategic Organization*, 9(2): 136–162.

Kostova, T. 1999. Transnational transfer of strategic organizational practices: A contextual perspective. *Academy of Management Review*, 24(2): 308–324.

Kostova, T., & Roth, K. 2002. Adoption of an organizational practice by subsidiaries of multinational corporations: Institutional and relational effects. *Academy of Management Journal*, 45(1): 215–233.

Kostova, T., Roth, K., & Dacin, M. T. 2008. Institutional theory in the study of multinational corporations: A critique and new directions. *Academy of Management Review*, 33(4): 994–1008.

Kostova, T., & Zaheer, S. 1999. Organizational legitimacy under conditions of complexity: The case of the multinational enterprise. *Academy of Management Review*, 24(1): 64–81.

Kraatz, M. S., & Block, E. S. 2008. Organizational implications of institutional pluralism. In R. Greenwood, C. Oliver, K. Sahlin, & R. Suddaby (Eds.), *The SAGE Handbook of Organizational Institutionalism*: 243–275. London: Sage.

Langley, A. 2009. Studying processes in and around organizations. In D. A. Buchanan, & A. Bryman (Eds.), *The Sage Handbook of Organizational Research Methods*: 409–429. London: Sage.

Latour, B. 1986. The powers of association. In J. Law (Ed.), *Power, Action and Belief: A New Sociology of Knowledge*: 264–280. Keele: Methuen.

Latour, B. 2005. *Reassembling the Social: An Introduction to Actor-Network-Theory*. New York: Oxford University Press.

Lawrence, T. B. 1999. Institutional strategy. *Journal of Management*, 25(2): 161–188.

Lawrence, T. B., Leca, B., & Suddaby, R. (Eds.). 2009. *Institutional Work: Actors and Agency in Institutional Studies of Organizations*. Cambridge: Cambridge University Press.

Lawrence, T. B., Leca, B., & Zilber, T. B. 2013. Institutional work: Current research, new directions and overlooked issues. *Organization Studies*, 34(8): 1023–1033.

Lawrence, T. B., & Phillips, N. 2004. From Moby Dick to Free Willy: Macro-cultural discourse and institutional entrepreneurship in emerging institutional fields. *Organization*, 11(5): 689–711.

Lawrence, T. B., & Suddaby, R. 2006. Institutions and institutional work. In S. R. Clegg, C. Hardy, & T. Lawrence (Eds.), *Handbook of Organization Studies*, 2nd ed.: 215–255. London: Sage.

Lawrence, T. B., Suddaby, R., & Leca, B. 2011. Institutional work: Refocusing institutional studies of organization. *Journal of Management Inquiry*, 20(1): 52–58.

Leblebici, H., Salancik, G. R., Copay, A., & King, T. 1991. Institutional change and the transformation of interorganizational fields: An organizational history of the US radio broadcasting industry. *Administrative Science Quarterly*, 36: 333–363.

Lepak, D. P., Smith, K. G., & Taylor, M. S. 2007. Value creation and value capture: A multilevel perspective. *Academy of Management Review*, 32(1): 180–194.

Li, D., & Schoenherr, T. 2023. The institutionalization of sharing economy platforms in China. *Journal of Operations Management*, 69: 764–793.

Ligonie, M. 2018. The 'forced performativity' of a strategy concept: Exploring how shared value shaped a gambling company's strategy. *Long Range Planning*, 51: 463–479.

Lim, J. 2023. The balancing act of corporate political activity under institutional pressure. *Strategic Organization*, 21(4): 856–873.

Lok, J. 2010. Institutional logics as identity projects. *Academy of Management Journal*, 53(6): 1305–1335.

Lok, J., & de Rond, M. 2013. On the plasticity of institutions: Containing and restoring practice breakdowns at the Cambridge University Boat Club. *Academy of Management Journal*, 56(1): 185–207.

Lounsbury, M. 2001. Institutional sources of practice variation: Staffing college and university recycling programs. *Administrative Science Quarterly*, 46: 29–56.

Lounsbury, M. 2002. Institutional transformation and status mobility: The professionalization of the field of finance. *Academy of Management Journal*, 45(1): 255–266.

Lounsbury, M. 2007. A tale of two cities: Competing logics and practice variation in the professionalizing of mutual funds. *Academy of Management Journal*, 50(2): 289–307.

Lounsbury, M. 2008. Institutional rationality and practice variation: New directions in the institutional analysis of practice. *Accounting, Organizations and Society*, 33: 349–361.

Lounsbury, M., Anderson, D. A., & Spee, P. 2021. On practice and institution. In M. Lounsbury, D. A. Anderson, & P. Spee (Eds.), *On Practices and Institutions: Theorizing the Interface. Research in the Sociology of Organizations*, Vol. 70: 1–28. Bingley: Emerald.

Lounsbury, M., & Crumley, E. T. 2007. New practice creation: An institutional perspective on innovation. *Organization Studies*, 28(7): 993–1012.

Lounsbury, M., & Glynn, M. A. 2001. Cultural entrepreneurship: Stories, legitimacy, and the acquisition of resources. *Strategic Management Journal*, 22: 545–564.

Lounsbury, M., & Leblebici, H. 2004. The origins of strategic practice: Product diversification in the American mutual fund industry. *Strategic Organization*, 2(1): 65–90.

Lounsbury, M., & Rao, H. 2004. Sources of durability and change in market classifications: A study of the reconstitution of product categories in the American mutual fund industry, 1944–1985. *Social Forces*, 82(3): 969–999.

Lounsbury, M., Ventresca, M., & Hirsch, P. M. 2003. Social movements, field frames and industry emergence: A cultural-political perspective on US recycling. *Socio-Economic Review*, 1: 71–104.

Lukes, S. 1974. *Power: A Radical View*. London: Macmillan.

Luo, J., Chen, D., & Chen, J. 2021. Coming back and giving back: Transaction, institutional actors, and the paradox of peripheral influence. *Administrative Science Quarterly*, 66(1), 133–176.

Mackay, R. B., Chia, R., & Nair, A. K. 2021. Strategy-in-practices: A process philosophical approach to understanding strategy emergence and organizational outcomes. *Human Relations*, 74(9): 13337–11369.

MacKenzie, D., & Millo, Y. 2003. Constructing a market, performing theory: The historical sociology of a financial derivatives exchange. *American Journal of Sociology*, 109(1): 107–145.

Maguire, K., Hardy, C., & Lawrence, T. B. 2004. Institutional entrepreneurship in emerging fields: HIV/AIDS treatment advocacy in Canada. *Academy of Management Journal*, 47(5): 657–679.

Mahoney, J. T., & Pandian, J. R. 1992. The resource-based view within the conversation of strategic management. *Strategic Management Journal*, 13: 363–380.

Maitlis, S., & Lawrence, T. B. 2003. Orchestral manoeuvres in the dark: Understanding failure in organizational strategizing. *Journal of Management Studies*, 40(1): 109–139.

Mantere, S. 2008. Role expectations and middle manager strategic agency. *Journal of Management Studies*, 45(2): 294–316.

March, J. G., & Simon, H. A. 1958. *Organizations*. New York: Wiley.

Maurice, M. 1979. For a study of 'the societal effect': Universality and specificity in organisation research. In C. J. Lammers, & D. J. Hickson (Eds.), *Organizations Alike and Unlike*: 42–60. London: Routledge and Kegan Paul.

McCarthy, J. D., & Zald, M. N. 1977. Resource mobilization and social movements: A partial theory. *American Journal of Sociology*, 82(6): 1212–1241.

Mead, G. H. 1934. *Mind, Self, and Society*. Chicago: University of Chicago Press.

Mellahi, K., Frynas, J. G., Sun, P., & Siegel, D. 2016. A review of the nonmarket strategy literature: Toward a multi-theoretical integration. *Journal of Management*, 42(1): 143–173.

Merkus, S., Willems, T., & Veenswijk, M. 2019. Strategy implementation as performative practice: Reshaping organization into alignment with strategy. *Organization Management Journal*, 16(3): 140–155.

Meyer, J. W., & Rowan, B. 1977. Institutionalized organizations: Formal structure as myth and ceremony. *American Journal of Sociology*, 83(2): 340–363.

Meyer, K. E. 2001. Institutions, transaction costs, and entry mode choice in Eastern Europe. *Journal of International Business Studies*, 32(2): 357–367.

Meyer, K. E., Estrin, S., Bhaumik, S. K., & Peng, M. W. 2009. Institutions, resources, and entry strategies in emerging economies. *Strategic Management Journal*, 30: 61–80.

Meyer, K. E., & Peng, M. W. 2005. Probing theoretically into Central and Eastern Europe: Transactions, resources, and institutions. *Journal of International Business Studies*, 36: 600–621.

Meyer, M. W., & Zucker, L. G. 1989. *Permanently Failing Organizations*. Thousand Oaks, CA: Sage.

Micelotta, E. R., Lounsbury, M., & Greenwood, R. 2017. Pathways of institutional change: An integrative review and research agenda. *Journal of Management*, 43(6): 1885–1910.

Miles, R. E., & Snow, C. C. 1978. *Organization Strategy, Structure, and Process*. New York: McGraw-Hill.

Miller, D., & Friesen, P. H. 1984. *Organizations: A Quantum View*. Englewood Cliffs, NJ: Prentice Hall.

Mintzberg, H. 1979. *The Structure of Organizations*. Englewood Cliffs, NJ: Prentice-Hall.

Mintzberg, H. 1987. The strategy concept I: Five Ps for strategy. *California Management Review*, 30(1): 11–24.

Mintzberg, H., Waters, J. A., Pettigrew, A. M., & Butler, R. J. 1990. Studying deciding: An exchange of views between Mintzberg and Waters, Pettigrew, and Butler. *Organization Studies*, 11(1): 1–16.

Moorman, C. 2002. Consumer health under the scope. *Journal of Customer Research*, 29: 152–158.

Munir, K. A. 2005. The social construction of events: A study of institutional change in the photographic field. *Organization Studies*, 26(1): 93–112.

Munir, K. A., & Phillips, N. 2005. The birth of the 'Kodak moment': Institutional entrepreneurship and the adoption of new technologies. *Organization Studies*, 26(11): 1665–1687.

Mutch, A. 2007. Reflexivity and the institutional entrepreneur: A historical exploration. *Organization Studies*, 28(7): 1123–1140.

Narayanan, V. K., & Fahey, L. 1982. The micro-politics of strategy formulation. *Academy of Management Review*, 7(1): 25–34.

Nelson, R. R., & Winter, S. G. 1982. *An Evolutionary Theory of Economic Change*. Cambridge, MA: Harvard University Press.

Newman, K. L. 2000. Organizational transformation during institutional upheaval. *Academy of Management Review*, 25(3): 602–619.

North, D. C. 1986. The new institutional economics. *Journal of Institutional and Theoretical Economics (JITE)/Zeitschrift für die Gesamte Staatswissenschaft*, 142(1): 230–237.

North, D. C. 1990. *Institutions, Institutional Change and Economic Performance*. Cambridge: Cambridge University Press.

North, D. C. 1991. Institutions. *Journal of Economic Perspectives*, 5(1): 97–112.

Ocasio, W., & Gai, S. L. 2020. Institutions: Everywhere but not everything. *Journal of Management Inquiry*, 29(3): 262–271.

Oliver, C. 1991. Strategic responses to institutional processes. *Academy of Management Review*, 16(1): 145–179.

Oliver, C. 1992. The antecedents of deinstitutionalization. *Organization Studies*, 13(4): 563–588.

Oliver, C. 1997a. The influence of institutional and task environment relationships on organizational performance: The Canadian construction industry. *Journal of Management Studies*, 34(1): 99–124.

Oliver, C. 1997b. Sustainable competitive advantage: Combining institutional and resource-based views. *Strategic Management Journal*, 18: 697–713.

Pache, A.-C., & Santos, F. 2010. When worlds collide: The internal dynamics of organizational responses to conflicting institutional demands. *Academy of Management Review*, 35(3): 455–476.

Pajunen, K. 2008. Institutions and inflows of foreign direct investment: A fuzzy-set analysis. *Journal of International Business Studies*, 39: 652–669.

Peng, M. W. 2003. Institutional transitions and strategic choice. *Academy of Management Review*, 28(2): 275–296.

Peng, M. W. 2006. *Global Strategy*. Cincinnati, OH: South-Western Thomson.

Peng, M. W., & Heath, P. S. 1996. The growth of the firm in planned economies in transition: Institutions, organizations, and strategic choice. *Academy of Management Review*, 21(2): 492–528.

Peng, M. W., Wang, D. Y. L., & Jiang, Y. 2008. An institution-based view of international business strategy: A focus on emerging economies. *Journal of International Business Studies*, 39: 920–936.

Perkmann, M., & Spicer, A. 2008. How are management fashions institutionalized? The role of institutional work. *Human Relations*, 61(6): 811–844.

Pettigrew, A. M. 1985. *The Awakening Giant: Continuity and Change in ICI*. Oxford: Basil Blackwell.

Pettigrew, A. M. 1997. What is processual analysis? *Scandinavian Journal of Management*, 13(4): 337–348.

Pfeffer, J. 1981. *Power in Organizations*. Boston, MA: Pitman.

Porac, J. F., Thomas, H., & Baden-Fuller, C. 1989. Competitive groups as cognitive communities: The case of Scottish knitwear manufacturers. *Journal of Management Studies*, 26(4): 397–416.

Porter, M. E. 1980. *Competitive Strategy: Techniques for Analyzing Industries and Competitors*. New York: Free Press.

Porter, M. E. 1996. What is strategy? *Harvard Business Review*, 74 (November-December): 61–78.

Powell, W. W., & DiMaggio, P. J. (Eds.). 1991. *The New Institutionalism in Organizational Analysis*. Chicago: Chicago University Press.

Pozzebon, M. 2004. The influence of a structurationist view on strategic management research. *Journal of Management Studies*, 41(2): 247–272.

Prahalad, C. K., & Bettis, R. A. 1986. The dominant logic: A new linkage between diversity and performance. *Strategic Management Journal*, 7: 485–501.

Quatrone, P. 2015. Governing social orders, unfolding rationality, and Jesuit accounting practices: A procedural approach to institutional logics. *Administrative Science Quarterly*, 60: 411–445.

Quinn, J. B. 1980. *Strategies for Change: Logical Incrementalism*. Homewood, IL: Richard D Irwin.

Ranson, S., Hinings, C. R., & Greenwood, R. 1980. The structuring of organizational structures. *Administrative Science Quarterly*, 25: 1–17.

Rao, H., Monin, P., & Durand, R. 2003. Institutional change in Toque Ville: Nouvelle cuisine as an identity movement in French gastronomy. *American Journal of Sociology*, 108(4): 795–843.

Raviola, E., & Norbäck, M. 2013. Bringing technology and meaning into institutional work: Making news at an Italian business newspaper. *Organization Studies*, 34(8): 1171–1194.

Raynard, M., Johnson, G., & Greenwood, R. 2016. Institutional theory and strategic management. In M. Jenkins, & V. Ambrosini (Eds.), *Strategic Management: A Multiple-Perspective Approach*: 9–34. London: Red Globe Press.

Reay, T., Golden-Biddle, K., & Germann, K. 2006. Legitimizing a new role: Small wins and microprocesses of change. *Academy of Management Journal*, 49(5): 977–998.

Reay, T., & Hinings, C. R. 2005. The recomposition of an organizational field: Health care in Alberta. *Organization Studies*, 26(3): 351–384.

Reay, T., & Hinings, C. R. 2009. Managing the rivalry of competing institutional logics. *Organization Studies*, 30(6): 629–652.

Reinecke, J., & Lawrence, T. B. 2023. The role of temporality in institutional stabilization: A process view. *Academy of Management Review*, 48(4): 639–658.

Ritvala, T., & Kleymann, B. 2012. Scientists as midwives to cluster emergence: An institutional work framework. *Industry and Innovation*, 19(6): 477–497.

Robertson, M., Swan, J., & Newell, S. 1996. The role of networks in the diffusion of technological innovation. *Journal of Management Studies*, 33(3): 333–360.

Rojas, F. 2010. Power through institutional work: Acquiring academic authority in the 1968 third world strike. *Academy of Management Journal*, 53(6): 1263–1280.

Rouleau, L. 2005. Micro-practices of strategic sensemaking and sensegiving: How middle managers interpret and sell change every day. *Journal of Management Studies*, 42(7): 1413–1441.

Sahlin, K., & Wedlin, L. 2008. Circulating ideas: Imitation, translation and editing. In R. Greenwood, C. Oliver, K. Sahlin, & R. Suddaby (Eds.), *The SAGE Handbook of Organizational Institutionalism*: 218–242. London: Sage.

Samra-Fredericks, D. 2003. Strategizing as lived experience and strategists' everyday efforts to shape strategic direction. *Journal of Management Studies*, 40(1): 141–174.

Schatzki, T. R. 2001. Introduction. In T. R. Schatzki, K. Knorr-Cetina, & E. von Savigny (Eds.), *The Practice Turn in Contemporary Theory*: 1–14. London: Routledge.

Schatzki, T. R. 2002. *The Site of the Social: A Philosophical Exploration of the Constitution of Social Life and Change*. University Park: Pennsylvania State University Press.

Schatzki, T. R. 2005. The sites of organizations. *Organization Studies*, 26(3): 465–484.

Schatzki, T. R. 2006. On organizations as they happen. *Organization Studies*, 27(12): 1863–1873.

Schatzki, T. R. 2021. Forming alliances. In M. Lounsbury, D. A. Anderson, & P. Spee (Eds.), *On Practice and Institution: Theorizing the Interface. Research in the Sociology of Organizations*, Vol. 70: 119–137. Bingley: Emerald.

Scott, W. R. 1987. The adolescence of institutional theory. *Administrative Science Quarterly*, 32: 493–511.

Scott, W. R. 1992. *Organizations: Rational, Natural, and Open Systems*. Englewood Cliffs, NJ: Prentice-Hall.

Scott, W. R. 2014. *Institutions and Organizations* (4th ed.). London: Sage.

Seidl, D., & Whittington, R. 2014. Enlarging the strategy-as-practice research agenda: Towards taller and flatter ontologies. *Organization Studies*, 35(10): 1407–1421.

Selznick, P. 1949. *TVA and the Grass Roots*. Berkeley, CA: University of California Press.

Selznick, P. 1957. *Leadership in Administration: A Sociological Interpretation*. New York: Harper & Row.

Selznick, P. 1996. Institutionalism 'old' and 'new'. *Administrative Science Quarterly*, 41(2): 270–277.

Seo, M.-G., & Creed, W. E. D. 2002. Institutional contradictions, praxis, and institutional change: A dialectical perspective. *Academy of Management Review*, 27(2): 222–247.

Sevón, G. 1996. Organizational imitation in identity transformation. In B. Czarniawska, & G. Sevón (Eds.), *Translating Organizational Change*: 49–67. Berlin: Walter de Gruyter.

Sewell, W. H. 1992. A theory of structure: Duality, agency, and transformation. *American Journal of Sociology*, 98(1): 1–29.

Simon, H. A. 1947. *Administrative Behavior: A Study of Decision-Making Processes in Administrative Organizations*. New York: Macmillan.

Simon, H. A. 1957. *Models of Man: Social and Rational*. New York: John Wiley & Sons.

Slager, R., Gond, J.-P., & Moon, J. 2012. Standardization as institutional work: The regulatory power of a responsible investment standard. *Organization Studies*, 33(5–6): 763–790.

Smets, M., Aristidou, A., & Whittington, R. 2017. Towards a practice-driven institutionalism. In R. Greenwood, C. Oliver, T. B. Lawrence, & R. E. Meyer (Eds.), *The Sage Handbook of Organizational Institutionalism*, 2nd ed.: 365–391. London: Sage.

Smets, M., Greenwood, R., & Lounsbury, M. 2015a. An institutional perspective on strategy as practice. In D. Golsorkhi, L. Rouleau, D. Seidl, & E. Vaara (Eds.), *The Cambridge Handbook of Strategy as Practice*, 2nd ed.: 283–300. Cambridge: Cambridge University Press.

Smets, M., & Jarzabkowski, P. A. 2013. Reconstructing institutional complexity in practice: A relational model of institutional work and complexity. *Human Relations*, 66(10): 1279–1309.

Smets, M., Jarzabkowski, P. A., Burke, G. T., & Spee, P. 2015b. Reinsurance trading in Lloyd's of London: Balancing conflicting-yet-complementary logics in practice. *Academy of Management Journal*, 58(3): 932–970.

Smets, M., Morris, T., & Greenwood, R. 2012. From practice to field: A multilevel model of practice-driven institutional change. *Academy of Management Journal*, 55(4): 877–904.

Sminia, H. 2005. Strategy formation as layered discussion. *Scandinavian Journal of Management*, 21: 267–291.

Sminia, H. 2009. Process research in strategy formation: Theory, methodology and relevance. *International Journal of Management Reviews*, 11(1): 97–125.

Sminia, H. 2011. Institutional continuity and the Dutch construction industry fiddle. *Organization Studies*, 32(11): 1559–1585.

Sminia, H. 2022. *The Strategic Manager: Understanding Strategy in Practice* (3rd edn.). Abingdon: Routledge.

Sminia, H., & de Rond, M. 2012. Context and action in the transformation of strategy scholarship. *Journal of Management Studies*, 49(7): 1329–1349.

Sminia, H., & Valdovinos, F. S. 2022. Implementing strategy and avenues of access: A practice perspective. In A. Zuback, D. A. Tucker, O. Zwikael, K. Hughes, & S. A. Kirkpatrick (Eds.), *Effective Implementation of Transformation Strategies: How to Navigate the Strategy and Change Interface Successfully*: 65–88. Singapore: Palgrave Macmillan.

Smircich, L., & Morgan, G. 1982. Leadership: The management of meaning. *Journal of Applied Behavioral Science*, 18(3): 257–273.

Spender, J.-C. 1989. *Industry Recipes: An Enquiry into the Nature and Sources of Managerial Judgement*. Oxford: Basil Blackwell.

Suchman, M. C. 1995. Managing legitimacy: Strategic and institutional approaches. *Academy of Management Review*, 20(3): 571–610.

Suddaby, R., Bitektine, A., & Haack, P. 2017. Legitimacy. *Academy of Management Annals*, 11(1): 451–478.

Suddaby, R., & Greenwood, R. 2005. Rhetorical strategies of legitimacy. *Administrative Science Quarterly*, 50: 35–67.

Suddaby, R., Seidl, D., & Lê, J. K. 2013. Strategy-as-practice meets neo-institutional theory. *Strategic Organization*, 11(3): 329–344.

Thornton, P. H. 2002. The rise of the corporation in a craft industry: Conflict and conformity in institutional logics. *Academy of Management Journal*, 45(1): 81–101.

Thornton, P. H., Jones, C., & Kury, K. 2005. Institutional logics and institutional change: Transformation in accounting, architecture, and publishing. In C. Jones, & P. H. Thornton (Eds.), *Sociology in Organizations*: 125–170. London: JAI Press.

Thornton, P. H., & Ocasio, W. 1999. Institutional logics and the historical contingency of power in organizations: Executive succession in the higher education publishing industry, 1958–1990. *American Journal of Sociology*, 105(3): 801–843.

Thornton, P. H., & Ocasio, W. 2008. Institutional logics. In R. Greenwood, C. Oliver, K. Sahlin, & R. Suddaby (Eds.), *The SAGE Handbook of Organizational Institutionalism*: 99–129. London: Sage.

Thornton, P. H., Ocasio, W., & Lounsbury, M. 2012. *The Institutional Logics Perspective: A New Approach to Culture, Structure and Process*. Oxford: Oxford University Press.

Tolbert, P. S., & Zucker, L. G. 1983. Institutional sources of change in the formal structure of organizations: The diffusion of civil service reform, 1880–1935. *Administrative Science Quarterly*, 28: 22–39.

Tsoukas, H., & Chia, R. 2003. Everything flows and nothing abides. *Process Studies*, 32(2): 196–224.

Vaara, E., Kleymann, B., & Seristö, H. 2004. Strategies as discursive constructions: The case of airline alliances. *Journal of Management Studies*, 41(1): 1–35.

Välikangas, L., & Carlsen, A. 2020. Spitting in the salad: Minor rebellion as institutional agency. *Organization Studies*, 41(9): 543–561.

Van de Ven, A. H. 1992. Suggestions for studying strategy process: A research note. *Strategic Management Journal*, 13(Summer Special Issue): 169–191.

Vargha, Z. 2018. Performing a strategy's world: How redesigning customers made relationship banking possible. *Long Range Planning*, 51: 480–494.

Veblen, T. 1909. The limitations of marginal utility. *Journal of Political Economy*, 17(9): 620–636.

Von Mises, L. 1949. *Human Action*. Chicago, IL: Henry Regnery.

Voronov, M., & Vince, R. 2012. Integrating emotions into the analysis of institutional work. *Academy of Management Review*, 37(1): 58–81.

Weick, K. E. 1979. *The Social Psychology of Organizing* (2nd ed.). New York: Random House.

Weick, K. E. 1995. *Sensemaking in Organizations*. Thousand Oaks, CA: Sage.

Weick, K. E., Sutcliffe, K. M., & Obstfeld, D. 2005. Organizing and the process of sensemaking. *Organization Science*, 16(4): 409–421.

Whipp, R., & Clark, P. 1986. *Innovation and the Auto Industry*. London: Frances Pinter.

Whitley, R. D. 1990. Eastern Asian enterprise structures and the comparative analysis of forms of business organization. *Organization Studies*, 11(1): 47–74.

Whitley, R. D. 1991. The social construction of business systems in East Asia. *Organization Studies*, 12(1): 1–28.

Whitley, R. D. 1992. *European Business Systems: Firms and Markets in Their National Contexts*. London: Sage.

Whitley, R. D. 1994. Dominant forms of economic organization in market economies. *Organization Studies*, 15(2): 153–182.

Whitley, R. D. 1998. Internationalization and varieties of capitalism: The limited effects of cross-national coordination of economic activities on the nature of business systems. *Review of International Political Economy*, 5(3): 445–481.

Whitley, R. D. 1999. *Divergent Capitalisms: The Social Structuring and Change of Business Systems*. Oxford: Oxford University Press.

Whitley, R. D. 2000. The institutional structuring of innovation strategies: Business systems, firm types and patterns of technical change in different market economies. *Organization Studies*, 21(5): 855–886.

Whitley, R. D. 2003. From the search for universal correlations to institutional structuring of economic organization and change: The development and future of organization studies. *Organization*, 10(3): 481–501.

Whitley, R. D. 2007. *Business Systems and Organizational Capabilities*. Oxford: Oxford University Press.

Whittington, R. 2006. Completing the practice turn in strategy research. *Organization Studies*, 27(5): 613–634.

Whittington, R. 2015. Giddens, structuration theory and strategy as practice. In D. Golsorkhi, L. Rouleau, D. Seidl, & E. Vaara (Eds.), *The Cambridge Handbook of Strategy as Practice*, 2nd ed.: 145–164. Cambridge: Cambridge University Press.

Wijen, F., & Ansari, S. 2007. Overcoming inaction through collective institutional entrepreneurship: Insights from regime theory. *Organization Studies*, 28(7): 1079–1100.

Williamson, O. E. 1975. *Markets and Hierarchies*. New York: Free Press.

Williamson, O. E. 1981. The economics of organization: The transaction cost approach. *American Journal of Sociology*, 87(3): 548–577.

Williamson, O. E. 1991. Strategizing, economizing, and economic organization. *Strategic Management Journal*, 12(Winter Special Issue): 75–94.

Williamson, O. E. 1999a. Public and private bureaucracies: A transaction cost economics perspective. *Journal of Law, Economics & Organization*, 15(1): 306–342.

Williamson, O. E. 1999b. Strategy research: Governance and competitive perspectives. *Strategic Management Journal*, 20(12): 1087–1108.

Williamson, O. E. 2000. The new institutional economics: Taking stock, looking ahead. *Journal of Economic Literature*, 38(3): 595–613.

Woodward, J. 1965. *Industrial Organization: Theory and Practice*. Oxford: Oxford University Press.

Zajac, E. J., & Westphal, J. D. 2004. The social construction of market value: Institutionalization and learning perspectives on stock market reactions. *American Sociological Review*, 69(3): 433–457.

Zietsma, C., Groenewegen, P., Logue, D., & Hinings, C. R. 2017. Field or fields? Building the scaffolding for cumulation of research on institutional fields. *Academy of Management Annals*, 11(1): 391–450.

Zietsma, C., & Lawrence, T. B. 2010. Institutional work in the transformation of an organizational field: The interplay of boundary work and practice work. *Administrative Science Quarterly*, 55: 189–221.

Zilber, T. B. 2002. Institutionalization as an interplay between actions, meanings and actors: The case of a rape crisis center in Israel. *Academy of Management Journal*, 45(1): 234–254.

Zilber, T. B. 2006. The work of the symbolic in institutional processes: Translations of rational myths in Israeli high tech. *Academy of Management Journal*, 49(2): 281–303.

Zilber, T. B. 2024. Narrating institutional logics into effect: Coherence across cognitive, political, and emotional elements. *Administrative Science Quarterly*, 69(1), 172–221.

Zucker, L. G. 1983. Organizations as institutions. In S. B. Bacharach (Ed.), *Advances in Organizational Theory and Research*: 1–43. Greenwich, CN: JAI Press.

Cambridge Elements ≡

Business Strategy

J.-C. Spender
Kozminski University

J.-C. Spender is a research Professor, Kozminski University. He has been active in the business strategy field since 1971 and is the author or co-author of 7 books and numerous papers. His principal academic interest is in knowledge-based theories of the private sector firm, and managing them.

About the Series

Business strategy's reach is vast, and important too since wherever there is business activity there is strategizing. As a field, strategy has a long history from medieval and colonial times to today's developed and developing economies. This series offers a place for interesting and illuminating research including industry and corporate studies, strategizing in service industries, the arts, the public sector, and the new forms of Internet-based commerce. It also covers today's expanding gamut of analytic techniques.

Cambridge Elements ⹀

Business Strategy

Elements in the Series

Printed in the United States
by Baker & Taylor Publisher Services